Complete Book of the Man-for-Man Defense

Complete Book of the Man-for-Man Defense

Archie Porter

Parker Publishing Company, Inc.
West Nyack, New York

© 1975, *by*

PARKER PUBLISHING COMPANY, INC.

West Nyack, N.Y.

Library of Congress Cataloging in Publication Data

Porter, Archie,
    Complete book of the man-for-man defense.

    Includes index.
    1. Basketball--Defense. I. Title.
GV888.P6   796.32'32   75-17652
ISBN 0-13-157560-0

Printed in the United States of America

Dedicated to my family,
Elaine, Sharon, Rick, Mike, Linda and Sonya,
who through the years have sacrificed so greatly
in order that I might enjoy the luxury of
coaching.

How This Book Will Help
You Win More Games

The complete book on man-for-man basketball defense explains in detail a particular type of man-for-man defense. The philosophy behind this defense is outlined, as are the reasons for using this particular method of defense. The man-for-man defense is covered step by step from the individual standpoint, including stance, footwork and individual defensive assignments through the complete team or five-man defense. Common offensive situations frequently confronted are dealt with in detail. Special offensive situations for which a team must be prepared are also covered in this book. Every phase of defense from the defensive break and organization to the five-man team concept are included. Each defensive technique and method presented is accompanied by a complete explanation as to why the defense is played in this particular manner.

In most basketball literature, defense is given little attention. When defense is the subject of a book, all too often, the base is broad and includes a discussion of a variety of defenses running from zones and zone presses to multiple defenses, stunting defenses, combination defenses, and match-up defenses, with perhaps a mention of the man-for-man defenses.

Basketball coaches are interested in the *little things* that make a defense effective. This book gives the coach a detailed explanation of how to cope with every offensive situation his team will meet in the course of the season. Guidelines and rules are offered in an attempt to organize defensive thinking and simplify the teaching of the basic defense.

When the defense breaks down, would you as a coach like to know exactly what went wrong? Would you like to be able to place responsibility for each scoring opportunity afforded the opposition? Do you wish your defense could play an aggressive pressure-type game and at the same time protect the basket area against the close shots? Do you want your team to force offensive mistakes through defensive pressure without committing defensive mistakes which cost layups? Would you like your defense to make interceptions and steals without gambling and taking wild chances on defense? Would an aggressive defense complement your offense? Would you like your defense to put points on the scoreboard for your team? Would you feel more confident if you asked your team to vary their team defense at some stage of the game as opposed to calling on them to go into an altogether different defense? Does the opposition drive you out of your man-for-man defense with the shuffle? Do you play a zone as your primary defense because teaching the man-for-man defense is too difficult and time consuming? If the answer to most of these questions is yes, then this book should help you solve some of your problems.

Archie Porter

ACKNOWLEDGMENTS

It is difficult for a coach to recall and give credit to all the people that have influenced his philosophy and thinking in the development of a particular style of basketball. There are three men who, unknowingly, have had a tremendous influence on my basic defensive philosophy.

The first of these is the late Blair Gullion, former basketball coach at Washington University in St. Louis. His book, *Techniques and Tactics of Basketball Defense* has been my defensive "Bible" throughout my coaching career.

I have been fortunate enough to listen to Mr. Hank Iba lecture scores of times. The soundness of his ideas has been tested and proven effective over the years, not only by his great accomplishments, but also by hundreds of coaches who might be called his disciples.

One of the most successful high school coaches to coach in the state of Texas was Cotton Robinson. His thoroughness and dedication to the development of basketball in the Southwest has made Buna, Texas a household word among coaches in this area. His influence on the game continues to exist throughout the region even though his coaching career was cut short several years ago due to poor health.

Many coaches have contributed to my knowledge of the game of basketball. To the three outstanding men mentioned above I am particularly appreciative, especially for their willingness to share their knowledge and "secrets" with others. It is my wish to share whatever knowledge I have accumulated with other coaches in hopes that in some small way it might contribute to their effectiveness.

CONTENTS

KEY TO DIAGRAMS

Defensive player	X
Offensive player	O
Path of player	→
Path of pass	⇢
Path of dribbler	⌇→
Screen	O———┤
Double screen	O———┤ (double)
Position of ball	Ⓑ ②
Coach or manager	□

1

Establishing Defensive Objectives and Principles

Defense contributes more to winning basketball than any other area of the game. Second to defense in importance is rebounding. Defensive rebounding represents the most frequent method of gaining possession of the ball, and is considered a part of defense by most coaches. If the coach is convinced that defense is the most important aspect of the game of basketball, and that it contributes more toward winning than other phases of the game, it will greatly affect his organization and planning.

There is a story about the coach who was meeting with his young team for the first time. As he faced his squad with a basketball in his hand, he was reported to have said, "Men, this is a basketball." Then, pointing toward one of the goals on the court, he continued, "That iron ring is the goal, and the object of the game is to put the ball through the ring." This coach only told half of the story. At least 50 percent of the game is to keep the opponents from putting the ball in their goal. Like many sports, you attack one goal and defend the other. Defense consists of the combined efforts of all five players, working together as a cohesive unit, in attempting to stop or at least limit the scoring opportunities of the opponent.

A good tough defense pays off in many ways. A good defensive team will be in every game and will not be humiliated or embarrassed by lopsided scores. Those nights when the shots fail to drop or the offense is not functioning properly, the defense will keep you in the game. When two apparently equal teams meet, the team that plays good defense has a definite edge in its favor. Defense is a more consistent factor in the game than offense. A good defensive team usually plays tough defense night in and night out. Defense serves not only as a stabilizer, but it also allows a team to control the tempo of the game. A good defense seldom permits an easy basket to be scored on them.

Defensive Objectives

Every coach has his ideas of what a defense should accomplish. The objectives outlined by the coach and the priority given to each determine the kind of defense his team will play. The defense presented in this text is based on the following objectives.

The first defensive objective is to stop the cheap basket. A layup is a cheap basket. Most layups come as a result of an opponent's fast break, an offensive rebound and follow-up or tip-in shot, a drive by an opponent (usually on the baseline), a lob pass to the post, or as the result of a well-executed screen play. The second objective is to decrease the scoring opportunities that come from the medium jump shot. Each year the shooters improve and the chances of a team beating you with the 15 to 17 foot jump shot increase.

The third defensive objective is to apply pressure and utilize forcing techniques that will limit the offensive scoring opportunities and force the opposition to disrupt its regular pattern or style of play.

Finally, through sound defensive pressure, the defense attempts to force the offense into mistakes. This objective involves constantly maintaining the proper defensive stance and position, with special emphasis on alertness and readiness to take advantage of any mistakes the offense might make.

Principles of Defense

A team defense, to be effective, must be based on sound principles capable of coping with the many varied and complicated situations which will arise in the course of a season. The principle of objectives must constantly be referred to. The coach must evaluate his defense periodically in terms of the question, "Is the defense accomplishing the specific purposes for which it was designed?"

In the defensive scheme presented, no more defensive players are employed than are necessary to cope with the situation presented by the offense. By dispersing the personnel in such a manner, the defense can more effectively cut off passing lanes, recover loose balls, and apply constant defensive pressure to the opposition.

At the same time the defense is attempting to economize its forces, specific situations demand player concentration in certain areas, particularly near the basket, in order to stop the cheap basket.

The defense is required both to apply pressure and to sag off and guard the vulnerable basket area. The reaction of the players to the situation and its demands, and the speed and mobility with which they react will determine the limitations of the defense and the demands placed upon them.

Proper timing and execution are given priority over trying to surprise an opponent with an unorthodox defense. Consequently, the simplicity of the defensive plan is designed to insure that all of the players understand thoroughly the system of defense presented. The element of surprise is utilized by changing the point of attack and using variations of the basic defense.

Teamwork is the essence of a good defense. The cooperation and help that players give to each other determine the degree of success the defense will enjoy.

The application of sound principles is necessary to accomplish the desired objectives. Adherence to the principles outlined will be instrumental in developing a tough, hard-nosed, basically sound defense, and will make it possible to realize the predetermined objectives.

How Many Defenses?

The trend in the game of basketball is toward multiple defenses. It is not uncommon for a team to use half a dozen defenses in the course of a game. Many teams have ten or twelve different defenses in their repertoire. Usually these defenses take the form of various standard or dropback zones such as the 1-3-1, 3-2, 1-2-2, 2-3, and 2-1-2. Coaches have devised methods of extending these basic zone formations over half, three-quarters, and the full court. Signals and keys such as the score, the time remaining, and whether the offense scored a field goal, a free throw or did not score, are used as a basis for changing the defenses.

The ingenuity of coaches has shown up in the forms of unique defenses such as laning zones—that is, spreading the zone out over a large area and playing the passing lanes. More types of zone presses than ever conceived possible have become standard practice with many teams. Double-teaming and trapping is the rule rather than the exception in defensive teaching. The combination defenses are appearing with more regularity. Not only the box and one, the diamond and one, and the triangle and two, but new combinations of part zone and part man-for-man, such as four men playing man-for-man defense and the center playing a zone and guarding the basket area, are becoming standard procedure.

Clever coaches are constantly devising new combinations and new keys for changing the various combinations of man-for-man and zone within the team concept of defense. Special defenses for specific situations, such as defending against the out-of-bounds play, are common practice. Some teams go into an automatic defense when the ball is in a certain position on the court or when a certain player has possession of the ball.

Attempting to disguise or conceal a specific defense by making it appear to be another is a practice many teams employ to fool the offense. Such tactics as playing a zone with the players in the zone yelling "switch" each time the offensive players cross in front of them is an example of attempting to disguise a zone as a man-for-man defense. Teams that play a switching man-for-man defense will hustle back to their defensive goal and set up their defense with all five players having their arms spread, giving the appearance of a zone. When an offensive team has a special player designated to *check* the defense, the defense will let him cut through the defense unaccompanied by an assigned defensive player, causing him to direct the offense to set up their zone attack. When the offensive play-maker comes back outside to give directions, the defense goes into its regular man-for-man defense, hoping that the offense has been tricked into thinking it is attacking a zone defense. Teams that use a basic overload in attacking zone defenses can be fooled by playing the offensive man that goes to the corner to set up the overload man-for-man until he reaches the corner, then keying on his position to go into a zone.

Perhaps the most deceptive of the concealed defenses is the *match-up* defense. This defense usually sets up in a zone, then slyly slides from the basic zone into a coverage that matches the offensive set man-for-man. This defense has become increasingly popular in recent years and some coaches, after extensive experimentation, have devised methods of covering most offensive patterns with this defense, and use it as their basic defense.

The above discussion indicates some of the devices to which coaches have resorted in an effort to contain today's high-powered offenses. Modern coaches are not fearful of trying something new and different. As a matter of fact many coaches are convinced that unorthodox techniques and methods, simply because they are unorthodox, offer the best approach to defensive strategy. The coach is confronted with a decision of major importance: Which offers the best solution—multiple defense or a single primary defense? An unorthodox defense which will surprise the offense or a time-tested defensive plan which is capable of countering any offensive threat?

The philosophy presented in this book adheres to the principle of doing a few things well as opposed to inadequately presenting several defenses. It is planned that the primary defense will be used 75 percent to 90 percent of the time, and consequently defensive practice is proportioned in the same ratio. Should the tactical situation demand a change in defensive strategy, rather than change to a completely different defensive concept, the recommendation presented is one of utilizing a variation of the basic defense. The teaching and consequent new learning required in presenting variations of the basic defense is less demanding on the players, easier to learn, and more apt to be effective than some completely different presentation which violates the basic techniques already mastered. Coaches who run multiple defenses depend on the element of surprise to make their defense effective. A basic defense which is fundamentally sound and properly executed is offered as a better alternative.

Zone Defense or Man-for-Man Defense?

Many coaches are successfully employing a zone defense as their primary defense. It is important that the coach has knowledge of a specific nature to pass along to his team when the opponent's offense is giving them trouble. It is even more important that each member of the team has a complete comprehension of his particular responsibilities within the team defensive plan. It is much easier to place responsibilities and eliminate excuses and alibis when playing man-for-man defense.

Much has been written about the advantages and disadvantages of the man-for-man defense when this defense is being compared to the zone defense. In reality, it is doubtful if there is a true man-for-man or a true zone defense in existence today. Every coach employs principles he believes in from each defense, and the outcome is a combination defense peculiar to that particular coach.

One of the most frequently mentioned disadvantages of the man-for-man defense is that it is not effective against the screening offense. The major part of this book deals with how to handle screens. Losing a half step and having to get help from a teammate is preferred to having two offensive players in one defensive player's zone. This so called disadvantage will not hold up, because each year more teams are using screens against zone defenses. When a zone defender is blocked in such a way that he cannot defend his assigned area, the zone defense is forced to cover the open man with a defender assigned to another zone. This type of coverage by the zone defense will leave another area open for the offensive attack.

Some coaches insist that it is a disadvantage to play the man rather than the ball. Ideally, each defensive player should be in a position so that he can see both his man and the ball. Obviously, this position is preferred to either the man or the ball. The big disadvantage of watching the man only is that a defender guarding a player away from the ball will not be aware of his responsibility in helping teammates and in picking up loose men in the area of the basket. When the defender focuses his vision on the ball, the most likely way he will get hurt is for his assigned man to move to another position on the court without the defender's knowledge. A general rule to compensate for this possibility is: Any time you cannot see your assigned man, back up toward the basket, watching the ball, until he comes in view.

A disadvantage sometimes mentioned is that the man-for-man defense is physically more demanding and strenuous. This appears to be an advantage, since all too frequently, zone teams get the impression that they are to rest on defense. A poorly executed zone defense tends to produce lazy defenders. However, any defense, zone or man-for-man, when properly taught and executed will be both demanding and strenuous.

Since the man-for-man defense is usually more aggressive, the tendency is to foul more in this defense than when playing a zone. This tendency to foul can be overcome by constant practice on defensive footwork, the proper use of the hands on defense, combating screens, and maintaining proper defensive position. Most defensive fouls are committed by a player who is not in the proper defensive position. The player who commits unnecessary fouls is usually the man that loafs and takes shortcuts on defense. The defensive player who fails to adjust his position when the ball is passed or when his man moves will find himself out of position when he is called on to perform specific responsibilities in the team defense. A common example of a foolish foul occurs when the front line support man does not move far enough to provide help on the driver and consequently reaches in and grabs at the driver. Zone defenders have an even greater tendency to foul when the offense penetrates the zone, simply because they are not adept at the techniques of individual defense.

The advantage that the zone defense enjoys in better rebounding is often mentioned as one of the primary reasons for playing a zone. The zone defense can station its big players in areas under the basket so that they are in the proximity of the basket when the shot is taken. Opposed to this reasoning, one of the biggest advantages of the man-for-man defense is that each defensive player has an assigned opponent he is responsible for blocking off the boards when the shot is taken. It is easier to split two zone defenders and get a good offensive rebounding position than it is to get by a single defensive player who is adept at blocking out.

The major area in which the coach's influence has a bearing on the outcome of the game is that of the defensive match-up. The advantage of the man-for-man defense when it comes to matching speed against speed, size against size, etc., is undeniable. The coach can match his best defender against the opponent's star player, he can match the player who boxes out best against the opponent's best rebounder, he can match his quick aggressive defensive player against the opposition's best ball handler, and so on.

The man-for-man defense affords the advantage of placing responsibility where it belongs. Each time the opposition gets a good scoring opportunity, the coach and the team will know where the defensive breakdown occurred. This asset alone will do much to discourage the players from making excuses and alibis when their man scores. Advantages and disadvantages of both styles of defense are numerous, but one other major consideration favoring a man-for-man defense is dictated by the situation in which a team finds itself all too frequently—namely, the short end of the score in the late stages of a game. The zone defense is not the best type of defense to employ when you need possession of the ball. If a team is forced to resort to a man-for-man defense in the situation mentioned above, it seems logical that the chances of success would be greater if a well-practiced method of attack were employed. The advantages afforded by a zone defense make it mandatory that every team have some type of zone, as a secondary defense, in its repertoire.

2

Coaching Individual Man-for-Man Defensive Techniques

Individual defense is a prerequisite of a sound team defense. The individual must first develop a sound defensive stance, and then master certain movements in all directions while in the defensive stance. Proper footwork is the essence of sound defense. Each player must learn, within the team defensive concept, how to defend specific situations such as offensive fakes, guarding a dribbler, defensing the strong side forward, covering the offside guard, how to defense a player cutting through the defense, stopping the give and go, and guarding the flash post. Likewise, it is important that each individual has an understanding of the proper use of the hands, the voice, and the eyes while playing defense.

Stance

Most coaches are in agreement concerning the elements of the proper defensive stance. A good defensive stance involves having the feet spread, knees flexed with tail down, back straight, and head up. Normally, the feet are spread about shoulders' width apart. If a player can be comfortable and can move with a wider stance, it is preferable that the feet are slightly farther apart than the shoulders' width. The knees should be flexed with the tail down, and the weight evenly distributed on the base provided by the feet. The degree to which the knees are bent depends on the individual. Each player should determine what particular stance is comfortable for him. A low stance is best, but the player should determine the stance from which he can operate most effectively. The back should be straight and the head up. The line of the back should be almost perpendicular to the floor, thus ensuring that the head will be up and the vision will be increased. The body weight should be evenly distributed on both feet, thus affording better movement in any direction. A common defensive error in stance occurs when the defensive player raises his tail, thus bringing his back to a position horizontal to the floor, and consequently lowering the head. This position, with the head forward, limits the vision of the defensive player and distributes the body weight unevenly with too much weight forward. When the body weight is thus distributed, it is extremely difficult for the defensive player to move backward. Players should keep their heads above their belt buckles. This illustration of position affords body balance and body control, which will enable the player to move quickly in any direction. The particular situation confronting the defensive player and his abilities dictate which stance, staggered or parallel, will be used. Again, results are most important; the player should use the stance which is most effective for him.

Defensive Footwork

Footwork is the essence of good defense. A player must be able to move his feet in order to play sound defense. In early season practices quick movement of the feet can be emphasized by using the ten-second drill. With the team in a mass formation facing the coach the team is instructed to assume the proper defensive stance. Upon the instruction "go" from the coach, the players begin to move their feet up and down as quickly as possible in a "machine gun" type of motion; this motion is continued for ten seconds, at which time the coach instructs the players to "stop." The footwork involved in this drill is similar to running in place, except that the feet are lifted only slightly off the floor. The players are encouraged to see how many times they can touch the floor with their feet within the ten seconds allotted. During this time of movement the players are encouraged to maintain the proper defensive stance with such comments as "tail down," "back straight," "heads up," "feet spread," etc. At the end of ten seconds of movement the players are allotted ten seconds for a rest period, which is followed by ten seconds of movement, ten seconds of rest, etc. The ten-second drill is a very demanding drill, and the number of repetitions are increased daily up to a maximum of six to eight repetitions.

Approach Step

There are basic steps involved in defensive footwork which every player should master. The first of these steps is the approach step. This step involves a situation in which the defensive player finds himself some distance away from his assigned man when the offensive player receives the ball. The first concern in approaching the offensive player is that he does not drive to the basket. The defensive player must approach the man with the ball in a good defensive stance that will enable him to move in any direction. It is better, in this situation, to give the outside shot as opposed to taking a chance of getting beat on the drive. When the defensive player has a great distance to move in approaching his opponent, he may run several steps, but as he nears the offensive player, he must assume the defensive stance and have his body under control ready to move in any direction in order to prevent the drive.

The defensive player must be cautioned not to be outmaneuvered by an offensive player who uses the *fake-a-shot and drive move* in this situation. Generally, when approaching his man, the defensive player should approach on the sideline or baseline side of the offensive player. In the event that the offensive player should drive, he should be forced back to the middle and toward defensive teammates that can provide help.

A clever defensive move designed to draw the charging foul can be accomplished by approaching the offensive player slightly to one side; then, as the defensive man comes under control, make a complete stop and quickly hop in the opposite direction. Approaching the offensive player at this angle encourages him to drive opposite the line of approach. The defensive player must anticipate this move, stop and hop quickly opposite the line of approach, and have his defensive position established when the contact occurs.

Diagram 2-1 illustrates a basic drill designed for teaching the approach step. A defensive player is stationed under the basket with a

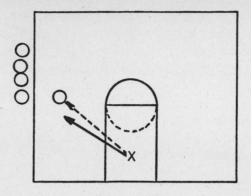

Diagram 2-1

basketball in his hand. He rolls the ball to the first player in the offensive line and quickly approaches him using the techniques just described. The offensive player may shoot the ball or fake a shot and drive. If the defensive player is able to attain the desired defensive position, then the drill becomes a game of one-on-one. In any drill of this nature, the defensive player is required to block out and rebound at the conclusion of the drill.

Attack Step

Another situation requiring basic defensive footwork exists when a defensive player finds himself in a normal position guarding a player in the scoring area who has not dribbled the basketball. The offensive player in this situation has at his disposal a variety of fakes and offensive maneuvers which he can use to beat the defensive man. These offensive moves include the rocker step with its variations, the fake-a-shot and drive, the fake-a-drive and shoot, faking one way and driving opposite, double fakes, and so on. The defensive player is caught in the dilemma of reacting to the offensive move. The defensive player should not react in the direction of the fake. When the offensive player fakes a drive, the defensive player should back up. The defensive problem in this situation involves preventing or pressuring the shot on the one hand, and at the same time, preventing the drive. The key to defensive movement is predicated by the position in which the offensive player is holding the basketball. Should the offensive player move the ball to eye level or shooting position, the defensive footwork involves moving close to the potential shooter. This footwork is referred to as the attack step. The attack step is accomplished by taking one hop toward the offensive player, keeping the same foot forward, and making certain that the feet do not get very far off the floor. The defensive player is now close to the offensive player in a staggered stance, with his hand raised at a 45 degree angle, knees still flexed, and his back heel on the floor. This pressure position will discourage the offensive player from shooting the basketball, and if not, will at least decrease his percentage from the field. With the basketball in the position described, the offensive player is not a threat to drive.

Retreat Step

When the offensive player moves the basketball to a lower level, a position from which he can execute a drive for the basket, the defensive player keys the movement of the ball and executes a retreat step. The retreat step involves hopping back to the normal defensive position again. It is important that the feet remain close to the floor, and that the same foot remains forward at the conclusion of the retreat step. A series of fakes by the offensive player would cause the defensive man to react with a series of attack and retreat steps depending upon the position of the basektball. Diagram 2-2 illustrates the attack step by the defensive player when the offensive man has the ball in the shooting position. Diagram 2-3 illustrates the position of the defensive player after executing the retreat step. Notice that the offensive player has the basketball in an offensive position from which he is a threat to drive.

Diagram 2-2

Diagram 2-3

Reverse-Retreat Step

A defensive player in a staggered stance can best protect in the direction of his rear foot; consequently, alert offensive players frequently attempt to drive in the direction of the defensive player's lead foot. When the offensive player drives in the direction of the defensive player's lead foot, it requires special defensive footwork which some coaches refer to as the reverse-retreat step. Assume that the defensive player has his left foot forward and the offensive player drives to the defensive man's left. This offensive move would require the defensive player to pivot on his rear, or his right foot, and to swing his left foot from the forward position, opening up and making his left foot his rear foot. From this point, should the dribbler continue in the same direction, the defensive player will have his left foot back and will be able to move in that direction. Should the dribbler reverse his dribble or change direction, the defensive player would again have to execute a reverse-retreat step by opening up and pivoting on his rear or left foot and swinging his right foot from the forward to the rear foot position.

Some coaches teach the reverse-retreat step against fakes toward the defensive player's forward foot. In most instances it is advantageous for the defensive player to have his outside or baseline foot back. This will enable him to protect against the baseline drive more effectively. Should the defender use the reverse-retreat step against fakes, the offensive player will be able to dictate the forward foot of the defensive player. Against fakes, the defensive player should retreat. Against a drive toward the forward foot, the guard should reverse-retreat and get in motion with the dribbler.

Guarding the Dribbler

In any pressure type of man-for-man defense it is imperative that the dribbler does not beat his assigned defensive player. When the dribbler whips his defensive man, the result will be a close unguarded jump shot or possibly even a layup. Defensively, five against four is impossible to cope with. Therefore, the primary rule in guarding the dribbler is *do not let him beat you*. It may appear to be contradictory that on the one hand pressure is applied to the dribbler, and on the other hand, the defensive players never let the dribbler beat them. The amount of pressure that the defensive player can apply will be determined by the quickness of the defensive player as opposed to the skills and quickness of the dribbler. The defensive player should apply all the pressure he can, but should not overpress or gamble or take chances, and above all, should not allow the dribbler to get by him. In reality, all that is required of the defensive player guarding the dribbler is that he maintain his position between the dribbler and the basket. To prevent the offense from getting an advantage in number by beating the defense with the dribble, each player must determine for himself the amount of pressure that he is capable of applying against a specific opponent. Some players, because of their lack of quickness, may have to bluff pressure while constantly giving ground. A one-on-one situation is the toughest situation in which a defender may find himself. A five-on-five situation is much easier for the defense to cope with. Team defense can control the offensive play through the use of special forcing techniques. The team concept insures cooperation and help from defensive teammates which further increases the defense's chances of coping with offensive strategy.

One-on-One Full-Court Drill

One-on-one full court is a good drill to practice defensing the dribbler. Early in the season the defensive player is instructed to maintain his position between the dribbler and the basket, and to make certain the dribbler does not beat him. This drill gives the defensive player an opportunity to evaluate his particular skills and quickness, and to determine the amount of pressure that he is able to effectively apply to the dribbler. As the season progresses, the defensive player in these one-on-one full-court drills is required to force the dribbler and see how many times, by overplaying, he can force the dribbler to change directions before he gets to the offensive end of the court. A defensive player's ability is evaluated by the number of times he can force the dribbler to change directions in this drill. On a full-court basis, should the dribbler beat the defensive player, the defensive player should sprint to a cut-off position and again assume the proper defensive stance.

While drilling on a one-on-one basis, it is advisable sometimes to station the defensive player on the ten-second line as the dribbler approaches. This type of situation occurs occasionally in the course of a game and occurs frequently if the defense is picking up at mid-court. The purpose of this drill is to teach the defensive player to get in motion as the dribbler approaches him. All too often the defender is caught flat-footed as the dribbler approaches, making it a simple task to dribble by him. The easiest player for a dribbler to beat is one that is standing still. The defensive player must get his feet moving before the dribbler reaches him, and he must be in motion as the dribbler arrives.

On a full-court basis, the dribbler should be forced to bring the ball down the side of the court. When the basketball is on the sideline, the directions in which it can be passed are limited. This position of the ball gives the defense an advantage in position on players away from the ball. When the basketball is in the middle of the court, the ball can be passed to the left or to the right, causing the pressure defense to spread'itself and cover more territory.

In guarding the dribbler, it is mandatory that the defensive player guard the man, not the ball. One of the most common mistakes the defender makes in this situation is to reach in and try to steal the ball from the dribbler. The guard should assume that the ball handler is a good dribbler and knows how to take care of the ball. The defensive player seldom can challenge the dribbler successfully, and to do so invites defensive mistakes. When the defensive player reaches for the ball, the usual result is that he commits an unnecessary foul, or he becomes off balance and the clever dribbler takes advantage of this to drive around him.

Should the dribbler become careless and fail to protect the basketball, of course the defensive player should take advantage of the dribbler's mistake. The defender should have the palms of his hands up, and motion made toward the ball should be cat-like slaps in an upward direction. By using upward strikes at the ball, the guard will not lose his balance. If the guard is moving alongside the dribbler, the motions toward the ball should be with the near hand and in the same direction that the dribbler is moving. If the defender swings the far hand toward the dribbler, a foul is almost certain to occur.

Many clever ball handlers use the reverse dribble in an effort to get past their guard. In order for this movement to be effective, the dribbler must move in close to the guard and get by him with a long step out of the pivot involved in the reverse dribble. Defensively, when the dribbler turns his back on the guard, the guard must retreat and put enough space between himself and the dribbler to prevent the leg cut.

When the dribbler is in the front court and has reached a point on the court where the foul line extended would meet the sideline, the defensive player should force the dribbler to the middle. The player guarding the dribbler has teammates in this area who are responsible for helping him. Expressions such as *cut him off* and *get outside* are used by the coach to encourage this defensive technique. Some defensive players are fundamentally sound enough and quick enough to encourage the dribbler to take the baseline and can then beat them to the cut-off position and draw the charging foul. Anytime a defender steps in front of an offensive player to take the foul, he must establish his position with both feet on the floor prior to the contact. There is always the possibility of injury when deliberately putting oneself in this position. The danger of getting hurt is greater when the defensive player is standing upright at the time of contact. The defender should be in an exaggerated stance with his tail very close to the floor when the contact occurs. This stance lessens the distance the defensive man will fall and controls the way in which he will hit the floor. The defensive player is allowed to protect himself with his hands and arms so long as he keeps them in close to his body.

Early season drills which will help teach the defensive footwork required to defense the ball handler under one-on-one are shown in the diagrams which follow.

Diagram 2-4 illustrates a one-on-one drill in which the offensive player, without a basketball, uses a change of pace, change of direction, and all kinds and combinations of fakes to get by the defensive player. The defensive player uses his footwork in an effort to maintain his nose-on-nose position with the offensive player and to keep the offensive player from getting to the basket. Notice in the diagram that

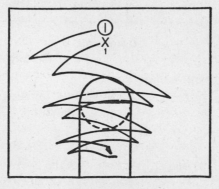

Diagram 2-4

the defensive player does not have to move as great a distance in order to maintain his position as the offensive player does in attempting to outmaneuver him. This drill is continued until contact occurs between the two players. When 1 makes his drive to the basket, X1 should position himself in the path of 1 and draw the charging foul. This drill can aid in developing confidence in the defensive players. The coach can point out the success they have had in keeping the offensive player from the basket when the offensive player does not have the ball, so it should be much easier for the defender when the offensive player is dribbling the ball.

Next is a one-on-one drill in which 1 is given a basketball and attempts to drive by X1 using all the offensive tools at his disposal. The defensive man is handicapped in this drill by not being permitted to use his hands. In Diagram 2-5, X1 is instructed to clasp his hands together behind his back. This drill emphasizes defensive footwork on the part of X1. Without using his hands, X1 tries to stop 1's attack toward the basket.

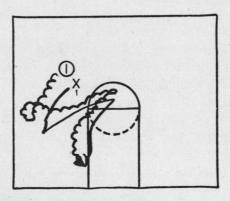

Diagram 2-5

Should 1 go up for a jump shot, X1 is to move in as close as he can get and apply pressure on the shooter by sticking his nose in the shooter's stomach on the shot. After the shot, X1 boxes 1 off the boards and gets the rebound.

One-on-one competition is one of the best drills for emphasizing defense. In order to make the most out of the drill, specific rules for the game are set up. The defensive player always hands the ball to the offensive player to start the drill. By beginning the game in this manner, the defense will always be ready to play and will not be caught by surprise. The sandlot rule that awards the ball to the man that scores also places a premium on good defense. Each time the ball is in-bounded, rather than beginning play from the spot in which the ball went out of bounds, it is brought back to the head of the circle. The play is resumed when the player on defense hands the ball to the offensive player.

As in all competitive drills, both offense and defense can be practiced. The offense can work on the rocker step and various other fakes, and the defense can practice the proper defensive footwork steps such as attack, retreat, etc.

When the ball handler kills his dribble, he should be aggressively attacked by the defensive player. The defensive man should move in so close and aggressively to the man with the ball that the ball handler becomes occupied with protecting the ball. If the defensive man can force the ball handler to pivot and turn his back to his teammates, he has done an excellent job. Practically all defensive plans involve putting pressure on the ball handler who has used his dribble, particularly when the offensive player is in the scoring area. The pressure defense herein described goes one step farther by putting pressure on the passer regardless of where on the court he may be located. This situation involving pressure on the offensive player who has used his dribble is referred to as *tight*. Each time the conditions described occur in practice, the coach should remind his players by yelling *tight*. The success the ball handler has in making his next pass is to a great extent determined by the amount of pressure the defensive man puts on him.

Defensing the Strong Side Forward

The forward on the same side of the court that the basketball is on is considered the strong side forward. The job of the defensive player that is assigned to guard him is to make him work to receive a pass. The defensive player should play his man in the three-quarter position. To explain the three-quarter position, split the difference between playing behind an offensive player and playing in front of him—this would be the one-half position beside the assigned player. If the defensive player moved half way from the one-half position toward the front position, he would be in the three-quarter position. The defensive player's knees should be slightly flexed, and his near hand should be in front of the offensive player to discourage or deflect a pass. The stance is closed, but the head is turned and the defender's eyes are on the ball.

The defensive player's responsibility is to make the offensive player move to receive a pass. The offensive player should not be allowed to receive a pass while he is stationary. The defensive player is coiled and alert, ready to take advantage of any offensive mistake. If the passer is careless and telegraphs his pass, if he lobs the ball hanging it in the air, if he throws a lazy slow-bounce pass, or if he passes to the wrong side of his teammate, the defensive player should intercept or at least deflect the pass. Each pass toward the basket or the baseline is pressured in the manner described above. The defensive player must not overplay to the extent that he gets beat with the backdoor play. One of the dangers involved in pressure defense is that if the defensive man meets with enough success, he begins to overpress and takes chances attempting more interceptions. The player defensing the strong side forward first has the responsibility of preventing the backdoor play and the subsequent layup or close jump shot. The defense is playing cat and mouse with the offense. It boils down to a matter of who is going to make the mistake first, the defense or the offense. The defense applies all the pressure it is capable of, but never so much that it overextends and makes a mistake. The defense tries to force mistakes, but not to the extent that it makes the mistake. Regardless of whether the mistake occurs as a result of defensive pressure or offensive carelessness, the defense must be ready to take advantage of it. Remember, the offense does not get any points for completing a pass. The defensive objective, when the offense is well-grounded in fundamentals, is to make the offense work to get open for a pass and to force them off their pattern or out of their offense even if only slightly. If the offensive player moves only a few feet to get open, the defense has gained an advantage. The offensive player did not receive the ball in the position in which he would have liked to receive it. The offensive player, being out of the desired position, will affect the offensive timing adversely and will usually force the next pass to be longer than desired.

Applying the desired pressure from the three-quarter position, and at the same time not permitting the forward to free himself for an easy basket on the backdoor cut, poses a defensive problem that requires a lot of attention. Coaches differ on the technique that should be used in defensing the cutback. Basically, the defender can retreat with the forward in one of two ways: (1) by opening up toward the ball, and watching the ball as he retreats, or (2) by closing his stance to the ball and facing his opponent as he breaks for the basket, focusing his attention on the man as opposed to the ball.

The biggest advantage to opening up toward the ball is that the defensive player is in a favorable position to intercept or deflect the pass to his man cutting behind him. If the offensive player fakes with his head and shoulders and does not move his feet, the defender can maintain his three-quarter position. If the offensive player moves toward the basket slowly, the defender can retreat and maintain his three-quarter position. When the offensive player fakes toward the ball, then cuts quickly for the basket, the defender may be able to maintain his three-quarter position for a step or two only. As soon as the cutter is out of the vision of the defensive man, the defensive player should pivot on his rear foot facing the ball, and make a quick hop toward the basket. The pivot and the hop combined will place the defensive man in or near the lane. Should the ball handler attempt to pass to the cutter, the defensive man will be in position to intercept. Diagram 2-6 illustrates the defensive footwork in opening up when the strong side forward cuts back. The footprints drawn with solid lines show the defender's original position. The broken-line footprints illustrate the position of the feet after the pivot is made. The shaded prints illustrate the position of the defensive man's feet after the pivot and hop are completed.

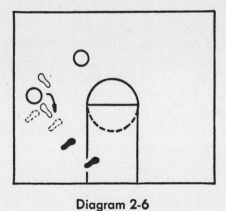

Diagram 2-6

The disadvantage of opening up to the ball is that momentarily after retreating to the basket the defensive player cannot see his assigned man and is susceptible to a quick move that might free him for a pass near the basket. When the forward cuts back-side and is no longer in the defensive man's field of vision, the defensive player retreats, facing the ball in the manner described. If the pass is attempted, he has a good chance to intercept. If the pass is not thrown, the defender must quickly find his assigned man and assume the proper defensive position. When opening up on the cutback, the offensive player can free himself for a pass, but that pass will not be near the basket for a layup. Diagram 2-7 illustrates the area that the offensive player must move to in order to get open. An advantage of opening up is that the defender is in a position to help, and he can see if a teammate needs help.

Diagram 2-7

When the defender faces his opponent as he cuts for the basket, he should retreat with his hands above his head and he should watch the eyes of the potential receiver for any indication of a pass. This method of defensing the cutback seems to be more natural for most players, but it has two distinct disadvantages. First, because the defensive player has his back to the ball, too frequently the pass goes by his head to the receiver who scores a layup. Secondly, should the ball handler drive, instead of passing the ball, the defender is not aware of the need to help his teammate. It is not uncommon to see an offensive player drive to the basket for a layup with a defensive player stationed under the goal, but not aware of action taking place because he is focusing his attention on his assigned man.

The opening-up coverage is favored when defensing the cutback since its disadvantages are fewer. However, both methods should be taught and the one that is most effective for the individual defensive player should be encouraged.

Diagram 2-8 illustrates the action of the weak side defensive forward when the cutback is being worked on the opposite side of the court. In the illustration, X3 is responsible for helping under the basket. In this instance X3 has a good opportunity to draw the charging foul if he will get in the lane and set his position. Also, 4 must be watching the ball, and many times will be unaware of X3's presence.

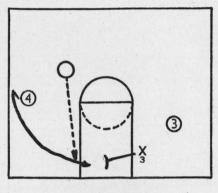

Diagram 2-8

Covering the Offside Guard

The basic rule, in defensing a player closer to the basket than the passer, is to pressure the receiver and make him move off his spot in order to receive the pass. Any pass away from the basket will be permitted, or even encouraged. The lateral pass across the court from one guard to the other is not considered a penetrating pass, and as a general rule is permitted. The primary responsibility of the man assigned to cover the guard without the ball is to be ready to help his teammate in the event the ball handler drives down the middle.

In Diagram 2-9, X1 must apply pressure on the ball handler. X2 covering the offside guard should apply all the pressure he can to 2, always remembering that his first responsibility is to help X1, should 1 drive to the middle. X1 is responsible for preventing 1 from driving down the sideline and should turn 1 into the middle so X2 can close the gate and prevent the dribbler, 1, from driving between himself and X1. X2 positions himself in such a manner that he can see his man, 2, and the ball. It is not necessary for X2 to station himself on the foul line, but he should be positioned in such a way that he can get to the cut-off

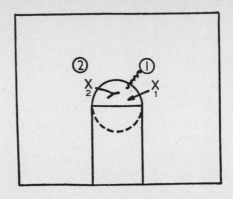

Diagram 2-9

position prior to the dribbler. Physically, X2 is close to his man, but mentally he should be prepared to help on the drive to the middle. X2 should, if necessary, come shoulder to shoulder with teammate X1. 1 is dribbling to the middle and, because he can see X2 drop off to help, and since 2 is within his vision span, 1 will, in most cases, pass the ball off to 2.

Diagram 2-10 illustrates the action of X2 when the ball is passed to his man 2. X2 must approach 2 in such a way as to prevent 2 from driving down the sideline. Coaching expressions such as *get outside* and *cut him off* are used to emphasize the proper position to X2.

The phrase *help and get back* describes the action taken by X2. This particular situation occurs frequently in the course of a ball game and must be practiced diligently. X2 can in some instances start to the

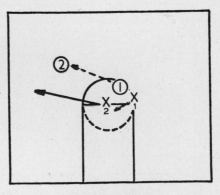

Diagram 2-10

cut-off position and by using defensive fakes, cause the driver to pick up his dribble. It is important that X2 only gives help in the amount needed by his teammate X1. Occasionally, X1 can control the drive to the middle and prevent the sideline drive also. In such cases it is not necessary for X2 to help, and he can close out on his assigned man, 2, and be alert to intercept the pass to 2.

Failing to slide far enough to keep 1 from splitting the defense, that is, driving between X2 and X1, is the worst mistake X2 can make. Helping when help is not needed, or giving more help than the situation dictates, is also a mistake. The second most common mistake X2 is apt to make is to help and then fail to get back to his own man quickly. Thus, the last part of the coaching point "help *and get back*." The instant 1 picks up his dribble, X2 should begin to move back to his assigned man. Stopping the dribbler is X2's primary responsibility and should provide adequate time for X1 to shape up on 1.

X2 and X1 do not switch men in this situation, nor do they double-team the dribbler. When X2 remains with the ball handler, he will give up the pass to 2 and an open shot. As X2 drops back to help, he should maintain an open stance so that 2 remains in his field of vision. Should 2 move into a different spot in order to get open for the pass from 1, it will be easier for X2 to find his man from the open stance.

In a situation where 1 has used his dribble, X2 has much more freedom. Diagram 2-11 illustrates the position of X2 when the dribbler 1 is dead. In the situation described, X2 can move out into the passing lane since the responsibility to help on the drive to the middle no longer

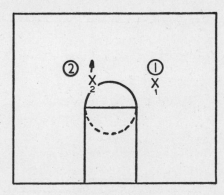

Diagram 2-11

exists. X1 should recognize the tight situation and apply pressure to the passer 1.

This discussion is predicated on the assumption that X1 forces 1 to the middle of the court. The sideline is treated in the same manner as the baseline and it is imperative that X1 does not let 1 drive between him and the sideline. Diagram 2-12 illustrates the importance of X1 overplaying 1 if necessary to keep him from driving down the sideline.

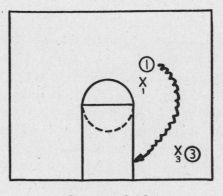

Diagram 2-12

X3 in the diagram has the responsibility of pressuring 3 in the event of a penetrating pass. It can readily be seen that X3 cannot be expected to defense the strong side forward in the manner previously described, and at the same time, be in a position to help X1 should 1 beat him to the outside. In order to effectively pressure the penetrating pass to the corner, X3 must be relieved of the additional responsibility of providing help on sideline drives. Consequently, X1 has the sole responsibility of preventing the sideline drive, and if necessary, must overplay his man 1 to the extent that 1 has but one direction to drive, and that is to the middle.

Stopping the Give and Go

The pass and break for the basket for the return pass, or *give and go* as it is better known, can be run in several ways. The give and go offensive play is particularly effective against certain defenses. This play is designed to work exceedingly well against a defensive player

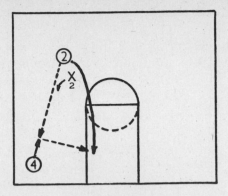

Diagram 2-13

who turns his head and watches the flight of the ball when it is passed. Diagram 2-13 shows how 2 passes to 4 and goes to the basket against X2 who is a swivel-head. Any time the passer can make a quick move and get between the ball and his defensive man, he will be open for a return pass on the give and go. In Diagram 2-14, X2 fails to adjust his position when the ball is passed, and 2 positions him for the return pass.

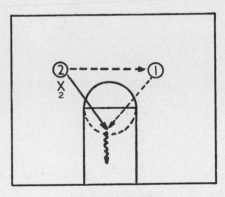

Diagram 2-14

Another of the common methods of running the give and go is for the passer, 2 in Diagram 2-15, to set up the defensive man with a fake opposite the pass, then execute a sharp change of direction to get position on the defender.

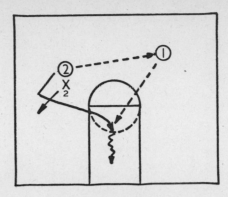

Diagram 2-15

Some offensive players use the bump and cut technique to get open on the give and go play. As shown in Diagram 2-16, 2 literally runs into his defensive man X2 causing X2 to break his stride and get off balance; then 2 cuts between the defender and the ball to open himself for the return pass.

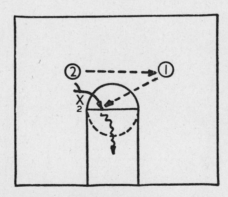

Diagram 2-16

The give and go is an excellent offensive weapon and is especially effective against pressure-type defenses. The defense must be prepared to stop this play. The technique used to neutralize this offensive maneuver is to teach the defensive player to back off his man and move in the direction of the ball immediately when his man passes the ball.

Diagram 2-17 shows the movement of X2 when 2 passes to 1.

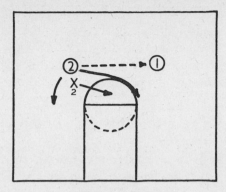

Diagram 2-17

With X2 in the adjusted position, 2 must do one of two things when he cuts to the basket: (1) run a wide rounded path as opposed to a sharp direct cut to the basket or (2) take a path behind X2. Forcing 2 to belly out on his cut to the basket will greatly reduce the effectiveness of the give and go. Should 2 elect to cut behind X2, then X2 is in the passing lane and should be in a favorable position to intercept or deflect the pass to 2. X2 follows the same rule the defensive forward used, namely, when your assigned man leaves your span of vision, back up toward the basket until he comes into your sight, then shape up in the proper defensive position. X2 would open up as he retreats, focusing his attention on the ball.

    Diagram 2-18 illustrates the movement of X2 when the ball is passed from the guard to the forward. Again, the cutter 2 is forced to

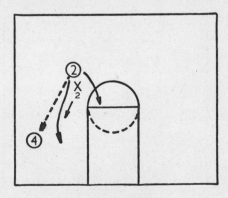

Diagram 2-18

belly out on his way to the basket, or to go behind the defensive player X2. X2 should position himself in such a way that he can see both his man and the ball. When his man is out of his view, he must retreat toward the basket until his man comes within his vision; then he must assume the proper defensive position for this adjustment.

Eliminating the Effectiveness of the Clear Out

The clear out is an offensive move designed to relocate certain defensive players to the advantage of the offense. The most common use of the clear out is to open up an area or even one side of the court in order to give a good one-on-one offensive player an opportunity to beat his man. Another effective use of this offensive movement involves clearing out anytime the defensive man is dropping off and helping on the post. The offense could also clear out the area behind the post man in order to make a lob pass into a post who is being fronted. Each of the situations mentioned is dealt with in later chapters, and each involves the overall team defensive plan.

The basic individual defensive method of guarding an offensive player who cuts through the defense is illustrated in Diagram 2-19. The clear out in many ways can be similar to the give and go. However, in most instances, the clear out man moves through the defense at a slower pace and usually is not expecting a return pass. X2 in the diagram must react in the direction of the pass in the same way he would on any pass since he does not know what to expect from the offense. X2 gives ground toward the baseline and toward the ball as it

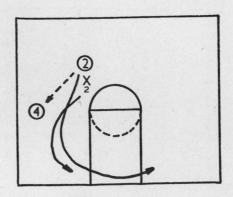

Diagram 2-19

is passed from 2 to 4. X2 is in position to help should 4 drive to the
middle. X2 will also force 2 to cut behind him. As 2 moves through the
defense, X2 moves with him, between him and the ball, and opened up
in such a way that he can see the ball at all times. X2 should *not* turn
his back on the ball and follow 2 as he cuts through the defense. When
X2 reaches the foul lane, he should stop momentarily to size the
situation up. A basic defensive rule comes into play at this point: *Do
not follow an offensive player who is moving away from the ball and
away from the basket*. Diagram 2-20 shows the point where X2 should
stop. There is no way at this instant that 2 can hurt the defense, so X2
stations himself in a position from which he can best help his teammates should the need arise.

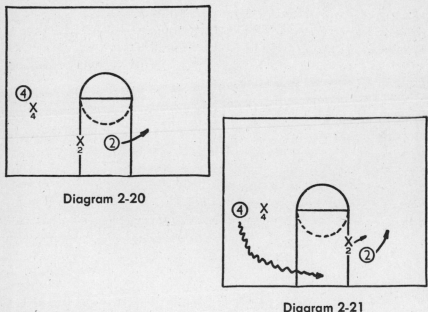

Diagram 2-20

Diagram 2-21

In the event 4 drove the baseline on X4, X2 would be in good
position to pick up the driver. One of the most glaring mistakes a
defensive player can make is to be close enough to help a teammate but
not be aware of the need for help. Diagram 2-21 illustrates what can
happen when X2 follows his man across the lane with his back to the
ball. The example illustrated in the diagram shows the reason why
emphasis is constantly placed on knowing where the ball is.

Guarding the Flash Post

A flash post refers to an offensive player stationed on the perimeter of the offense, who breaks into the lane or area usually filled by a stationary post man, to receive a pass. The offensive player could break into the middle from any position, but in most instances, he will break from a deep position on the side of the court away from the ball. The pressure defense is attempting to keep the ball from going into the post area. If the defense permits the pass to the flash post it becomes susceptible to the guard backdoor play shown in Diagram 2-22.

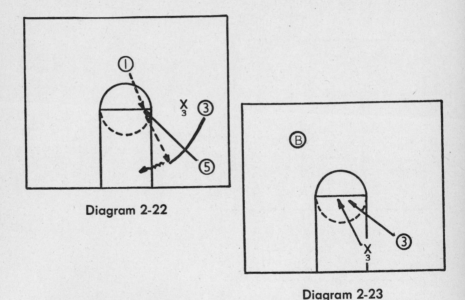

Diagram 2-22

Diagram 2-23

It is difficult indeed for X3 to play 3 in the three-quarter position when the ball is permitted to be passed into 5 breaking to the post.

In order to keep the flash post from getting open to receive the pass, the defensive man assigned to him must first assume the correct defensive position. X3 in Diagram 2-23 is in an open position and can see both the ball and his man 3. X3 must play close enough to prevent the direct pass to 3, but at the same time, must be aware of the possibility of 3 breaking up the lane. X3 is closer to the ball than the offensive player and should be able to beat him to the spot in which 3 hopes to receive the ball. Should 3 move out and set a stationary post, X3 would play him as a post man.

The offside offensive player who is breaking for the ball will normally execute a change of direction behind the defensive player when the defense fronts him as he moves in to the post area. Diagram 2-24 illustrates 3 making a cut behind X3. X3 should have his left foot forward and his left hand out and be between 3 and the ball when 3 changes direction and goes behind X3. X3 should pivot on his right (back) foot, and drop his left foot back opening up to the ball as shown in Diagram 2-25. From this point X3 shapes up in the proper post defense, which would involve moving in front of 3 and ending up playing him in the three-quarter position shown in Diagram 2-26.

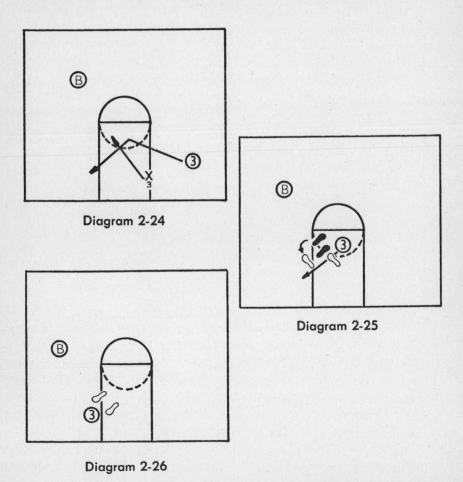

Diagram 2-24

Diagram 2-25

Diagram 2-26

The offensive player may move from any position into the post area. The defensive player should anticipate where he expects his man to move and to beat him to that spot. If the defender moves as though he were on offense, he will generally make it difficult for the flash post to receive the ball in the desired position. It is a basic rule on offense to change directions and cut back toward the goal when the defense beats you to the ball. Again, as it has been consistently stressed in all similar situations, the defensive man opens up and faces the ball as he adjusts his position against this offensive move.

The Use of the Hands on Defense

The position in which the offensive player holds the ball will determine the hand position when defensing a player who still has his dribble. The defensive player will raise the hand of his forward foot and move in close when the offensive player has the ball in shooting position. The defensive player will have his hands in front of him with palms up when in a normal defensive position. If the ball handler is careless and fails to protect the basketball, the defender should use quick, cat-like motions slapping up at the ball. Swinging up will help to avoid fouls and make it possible for the defensive player to maintain his balance as he goes for the ball.

The defense should move in and aggressively apply pressure when the offensive man has used his dribble. In cases where the dribbler is dead, the defensive man should keep his hands in the *plane of the ball*, making every effort to deflect the pass.

Play the man, not the ball is the rule for guarding the dribbler. Should the situation demand that the defense go after the ball, the defensive player should slide along beside the dribbler and slap at the ball with the inside hand, using motions away from the dribbler to avoid fouling. The hand should be positioned near the floor so he will have two opportunities to hit the ball—one as it goes down, and one as the ball comes back up to the dribbler's hand. When the defensive man overplays the dribbler and forces him to change directions, he will have an opportunity to deflect the dribble if he will position the hand nearest the dribbler close to the floor. Occasionally, the dribbler will place the ball directly in his hand on the change over.

Each potential pass receiver who is closer to the basket than the ball should play in the three-quarter defensive position. Each defensive player should have both arms up if he is on the opposite side of the floor from the play. The arm and hand position and motion can present not only a strong physical barrier for the passer, but a psychological one as well. The image or picture that the passer sees will often discourage passes to open teammates.

The proper use of the hands when helping or closing the gate causes problems with inexperienced players. The tendency is for the helping man to move part of the way to the proper support position and to reach and grab at the ball as the dribbler drives between him and his teammate. The extent to which the defensive players are encouraged to go after the ball depends largely on the officials in a given game. Another consideration worthy of mention is the number of team fouls which have been committed. It might be advisable to play more aggressively and to use the hand more freely prior to the time the opponents are allowed to shoot the bonus free throw.

The Role of the Voice on Defense

The best defensive teams *talk*. There is always action on the court by the offensive team that should provide the defense with plenty to talk about. For some strange reason it is difficult for the coach to get his defense in the habit of talking continuously. Specific terminology should be developed in order to avoid any misunderstanding regarding communications between players. The coach should insist that these terms be used daily in all drills and scrimmages.

As the team changes from offense to defense, the first man back should pick up the first offensive player on the attack and should point at him and inform the other members of the team "I've got him." This communication will aid his teammates in determining who has been picked up and who has not. The first two defenders back that are outnumbered by the offense must communicate in order to insure that the ball and the basket are covered. One of the two defenders calls out "I've got the ball, I've got the ball." The other responds with "I've got the hole."

Just as the offensive players yell "ball" when an interception takes place, the defensive players must encourage each other to hustle back and pick up their men with such expressions as "back, back" or "defense" when they lose possession of the ball.

Constant encouragement and reminders should be exchanged

among the defensive team members. Failure of a teammate to get his hands up and bother a shooter might be corrected by a prodding teammate yelling "hands," or "hands up." It is difficult to get all five defensive players to quickly recognize that situation when the dribbler is dead. Those that are aware of the situation can remind the others by shouting "tight!" The defensive post man has much more security when he hears a teammate yelling "you've got help" or "I've got the lob." The defensive man farthest from the ball is usually in a good position to see the entire playing area. From this vantage point he is the logical player to keep his teammates informed as to what to expect and the necessary adjustments.

The most important place to communicate in the defensive plan is that which involves combating screens. The defensive player guarding the screener should always warn his teammate of the impending screen. Such expressions as "watch the screen," or "screen right," or "screen left" can be used. "Slide through" or "fight through" are terms that can enable the two defensive players to reduce mistakes. "Help!" is a term that should be used when a player knows he has been screened and is in trouble. "I've got him" would indicate that the man responsible for helping can release and take care of his assigned man. Each time a defensive player in trouble is helped by one of his teammates, and the help saves a basket, the man receiving the help should acknowledge it with "good help" or "thanks." Talking will result in better coordination of the defense as well as increased cooperation among the team members. Communications will encourage mental alertness and breed the confidence that is required to develop championship-caliber defense.

The Use of Vision on Defense

The proper use of vision on defense gives the players something to talk about. The situations cited above concerning communications would be worthless if the individuals in a team defense did not *see* and size up the situations that warrant talking.

As the team changes from offense to defense, each member of the team should be concerned with two things as he retreats to the predetermined pick-up area. These two things are his assigned man and the ball. Many players leisurely trot back on defense with their heads down, seeing only the floor area immediately in front of them. Upon losing possession, each player should sprint to the area on the court where he is to pick up his man. Should he be the first man back, he should run backwards as he retreats. By running backwards he can see the other nine players on the court and the basketball. This position gives him a good vantage point from which to direct traffic and from which to help his teammates get into position on their assigned players.

All types of pressure defenses are based on the players' ability to perceive the situation and to anticipate the next move. Those defenses that involve double-teaming and cutting off the passing lanes cannot be executed without visual perception. The *tight* situation previously mentioned cannot be properly timed and executed unless all players are using their vision to recognize the situation. It is impossible to communicate to teammates regarding impending screens unless the screens are seen by teammates. The back man or safety in the pressing defenses and the man farthest from the ball in standard defenses are in the most favorable position to see the overall pictures. If these players have a thorough knowledge of the defensive plan and have been trained to recognize special situations, they will be able to communicate information to their teammates that will make the defense function with greater success.

Ideally, the defensive player should always be in a position such that he can see both his man and the ball. Anytime a situation on the court occurs such that he is not able to see both his man and the ball, he should adjust and focus his attention on the ball while at the same time retreating toward the basket until his assigned man comes within his span of vision. Playing the ball first will give the defense opportunities to intercept long passes, to help teammates when help is needed, to pick up loose cutters, and to recover loose balls in their proximity. The phrase "play with vision" is a coaching point that covers a multitude of common errors both offensively and defensively.

Blocking Shots

The dominance of so many tall players in the modern game of basketball has caused a drastic change in the defensive philosophy of many coaches. Defensive rules such as "never leave your feet" are outmoded. Because of the height, arm span, jumping ability and coordination of many tall players, it is becoming a more acceptable practice to play behind the post, let him receive the ball, then attempt to block his shot. It is not uncommon to see a team with a shot blocker play what amounts to a one-man zone. The big man is responsible for the area near the basket and his man. He is always ready to pick up any cutter or driver near the basket. Should the ball be passed to his man, he can approach him and apply pressure and perhaps still block his shot. Playing one man in this fashion relieves the other defensive players of much of their responsibility and allows them to apply extra pressure and to take more chances on defense. Coaches who basically do not believe in the zone press find themselves using this defense because of the capability of one player to protect the goal. The presence of the "goalie" in basketball has also influenced the type of offensive games used. Most offenses are no longer designed to produce a layup but rather hope to get a scoring opportunity from the medium jump shot range. This makes sense, because the layup is no longer the easiest or the highest percentage shot. The presence of the big man under the basket provides greater freedom for his teammates to attempt to block shots too. The outside defenders are aware of the security the big man provides in the event they get faked out, and the opponent gets by them.

One of the most frequent mistakes a young player will make is to jump too soon. If the shooter has his feet on the floor, the defender must wait until the ball leaves the shooter's hand before he jumps. The defender should jump straight up in the air and come straight down. Jumping forward will cause him to jump into the shooter and commit a foul. When the shooter jumps, the defensive man can jump. Many shot blockers enjoy slamming the ball out of bounds when they block a shot. Knocking the shot out of bounds can psychologically affect the shooter, but the shooter's team gets the ball right back. It is much better to block and retrieve the ball when the shot is taken. The shot blocker's teammates should be alerted to pick up the loose ball after the block. The defensive player, blocking the shot, should extend his arm straight up in the air and move in, under control, toward the shooter. Let the shooter shoot the ball into your hand. Many players follow through in a downward motion after blocking the shot or attempting to block the shot. This downward motion frequently causes contact with the shooter and results in an unnecessary foul. When the ball handler has used his dribble, the defensive man can attack the shooter more aggressively since he does not have to concern himself with protecting against the drive.

The tall player, who possesses shot blocking potential, should adjust his position in such a way that the ball handler is directly in front of him. As long as the big man can square off and keep the ball in front of him, he is a threat to block the shot and is much less apt to foul. The big man, who is in the middle of the defense and assumes the responsibility for the basket area as well as his assigned man, should try to stay on a line between the ball and the goal. This location will place him in a favorable position to pick up drivers coming into the middle or down the baseline.

An occasional goal-tending call will be offset by the psychological advantage gained through blocking shots. The big man should avoid backing up toward the goal and playing the ball as it nears the rim of the basket when the shot is taken from eight to ten feet from the basket. Playing the ball on its downward flight in this manner is goal tending even though it may not be called on every shot. The shot blocker should attack the shooter and attempt to block the shot as it leaves his hands on the close-in jump shots.

Many times the shot is blocked and recovered by the shooter or his teammate for the second shot. When the big man jumps to block a shot, he should come down with his feet spread, his knees flexed, and his arms up, ready to attempt to block the second shot.

3

Principles of the Man-for-Man Defense

The principle of simplicity can best be served by developing guidelines that reduce the number of defensive techniques to a minimum. Defensive techniques are often predicated on the location on the court in which the action occurs. The designation of special areas serve as a tool to aid the players in determining what to do in relation to where they are on the court.

The Scoring Area

The closer the shooter is to the basket the higher his field goal percentage will be. This statement influences many coaches in designing their primary defense. Basically, this statement is valid, but in many cases the advent of the tall defensive post man guarding the basket has made the close shots more difficult than shots from out on the court. Some players are spot shooters and can hit better from their favorite area than from closer in. Also, there are many individual exceptions of players who are long-shot specialists.

The trend in offensive basketball seems to be for a team to play for the medium jump shot. Team defenses normally include some plan to protect the basket area, and consequently, the offensive strategy dictates the use of plays that are designed to produce a medium jump shot. The point in this discussion is that one of the primary objectives of defense in today's game is to include some planned method of dealing with those scoring opportunities that come within a 17 to 20 foot radius of the basket. It is quite possible that more games are lost as a result of the shots made from this area than from those made underneath the goal. This area referred to as the scoring area is illustrated in Diagram 3-1. The scoring area is established early in the season by actually marking it on the court with strips of tape, about one foot in length, spaced approximately one foot apart. As the practice season progresses, alternate strips of the tape are removed until just prior to the first game when all of the tape is taken up. Hopefully, by this time, the players have become thoroughly familiar with the scoring area. The designated scoring area is varied for different opponents depending upon their shooting range. The designated scoring area can also be adjusted to meet the special ability of individual shooters.

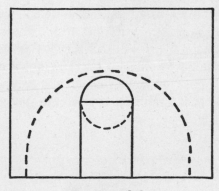

Diagram 3-1

The scoring area is particularily important as it applies to defensing screening plays. The method of defensing screens, in the vast majority of cases, is reduced to two possibilities. These options are: (1) fighting over the top of the screen and (2) sliding through the screen. The correct choice of these options depends on the location on the court in which the screen is taking place. Inside the designated scoring area the defense fights over the top of the screen. Outside the scoring area the defense slides through the screen. Any of the defensive players can be involved in defensing screens and it is vitally important that all players understand where they are on the court at all times. The detailed explanation of the techniques involved in defensing screens is treated in Chapter 8.

In the man-for-man defense a player's assigned man must be guarded differently in the scoring area than he would outside this area. The defense sometimes has time and space to recover from a mistake committed outside the scoring area, whereas, mistakes made in the scoring area usually result in a scoring opportunity. In general terms, the closer an offensive player is to the basket, the more difficult the defense should make it for him to receive the basketball.

The defensive position on the shooter must be closer and more aggressive as the shooter nears the basket. Regardless of the specific defensive plan, the defense must realize that when it is pushed back into the scoring area, the opposition is in sacred territory. When the defense retreats inside this area, it must tighten its belt, roll up its sleeves and be prepared to go to battle.

The standard dropback defense is designed to put pressure on the ball as it reaches the scoring area. The defenses are numbered, as illustrated in Diagram 3-2, according to the predetermined point at which the defensive players will pick up their assigned men. For example, if the defensive plan for a particular game is to play a half-court pressure defense, the number of that defense would be 50. The standard dropback defense is number ten. A three-quarter court defense is

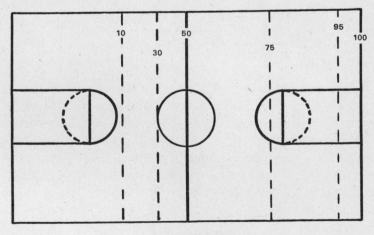

Diagram 3-2

number 75. The number 95 is used to denote a full-court defense, and 100 signifies a full-court defense which will press out or try to deny the pass inbounds. Each of these variations of the basic defense will be discussed in Chapter 10. Regardless of the point at which the defense picks up, a good offensive team will be able to move the ball into their front court and set up their offense. The defense could be playing 75 and be forced back into their ten defense. The defensive team ends up playing the standard dropback defense more often than the others, and for this reason, the illustrations and explanations will refer to the ten defense.

The Basket Area

That area near the basket must be defended at all cost. The defense should make every effort to prevent a player from receiving the basketball in this area. This area should be jammed in order to prevent offensive players from driving to the basket. In spite of all defensive efforts to the contrary, the offense will, on occasion, still be able to pass or dribble the ball into the basket area. The shaded area in Diagram 3-3 illustrates that special portion of the court referred to as the basket area.

The deeper the ball is toward the baseline, the nearer to the baseline all five defensive players should be. The defense has made a mistake when it allows the ball to penetrate the basket area. The defense can recover from this mistake if it forces the offense to pass the ball back out of the basket area.

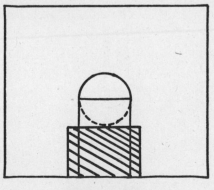

Diagram 3-3

The most frequent offensive methods for getting the ball into the basket area are: (1) the baseline drive, (2) the drive down the middle, (3) the post drive and (4) the lob pass to the post. Each time the ball gets into the basket area, the defense must use all tactics at its disposal to do one of the following: (1) make the offense pass the ball back out, (2) tie up the ball handler and gain a held ball, (3) deflect or steal the pass or dribble and (4) cause a three-second violation.

Diagram 3-4 illustrates the defensive adjustment when the offensive player drives the baseline. X4 fails to get outside and take care of the baseline. X5, the defensive post man, picks up all drivers. X2 has dropped off to the line of the ball in order to be ready to help in the event 4 drives to the middle. Since 4 went baseline and X5 has picked him up, X2 plays the return pass to 5 when 5 holds his position. If 5 should roll down the lane in front of the basket, X3 will play the pass from 4 to 5. X1, who is also on the line of the ball, rotates to cover the under-the-basket pass from 4 to 3. X4 stays with 4 even though he is out of position. When X5 stops the drive, X5 and X4 double-team 4.

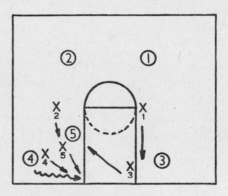

Diagram 3-4

The defensive adjustments made when the offense drives down the middle are shown in Diagram 3-5. X2 is playing outside 2, and 2 drives to the middle. X1 fails to give the proper help, and 2 splits the defensive players, X2 and X1, with his dribble. X5 always picks up the driver, as shown in the diagram. Notice that X5 moves laterally to stop 2. In other words, X5 lets the dribbler come to him; he does not help away from the basket. Moving away from the basket to help forces quick offensive reaction and does not allow X3 and X4 time enough to

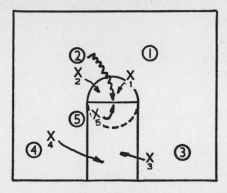

Diagram 3-5

rctreat into the lane. X3 and X4 provide the last line of support and must recognize the need for their presence under the basket with the ball at the foul line. 3 and 4 will be left open for a pass from 2, but this is desirable to the alternative of leaving 5 open under the basket for a pass from 2.

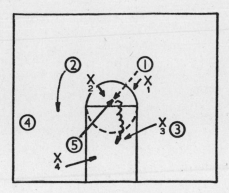

Diagram 3-6

An offense that has a post man who is an exceptional driver will move him out of his normal position far enough so that he can receive the pass, and then depend on him to use his driving ability to score. When the ball goes into the post, the deep defenders must react toward the basket in order to help on the driver or to pick up loose cutters. X3 and X4 loosen up, as shown in Diagram 3-6, when 5 receives the ball.

Diagram 3-7 shows the ball going into the basket area via the lob pass and subsequent defensive adjustment. X5 should move with 5 as he goes to the basket. X3 moves over to help on the lob. X1 rotates and checks 3. While the ball is in the air, X4 and X2 retreat as quickly as possible to the basket area in order to help if they can.

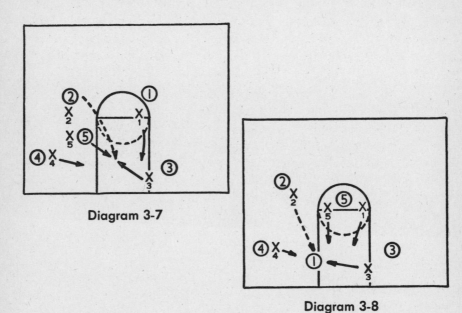

Diagram 3-7

Diagram 3-8

Occasionally, a defensive player gets screened completely out of the play or otherwise loses his man. If an offensive player, open under the basket, receives the ball, the nearest defensive man or men must take him immediately. The rule is to cover the man with the ball and depend upon your teammates to pick up your man. Diagram 3-8 illustrates the "ganging" technique when 1 evades X1.

The Middle Area

The third area on the court which requires special defensive concern is called the middle area or simply the middle. A defensive rule that prevents the defense from having to face many difficult situations is expressed in the coaching point, "Keep the ball out of the middle." Once the ball is in the middle, the coaching point becomes, "Force the ball out of the middle."

The middle area is an imaginary line which is an extension of the free throw lane as shown in Diagram 3-9. The middle area begins at that predetermined point at which the defense will pick up their men and continues toward the basket until it meets the basket area. For example, in a 50 defense the middle area would extend to mid-court; in a ten defense the middle area would begin a stride past the head of the circle.

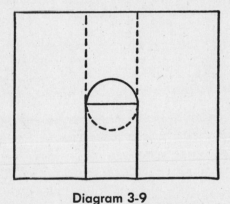

Diagram 3-9

Why is it important for the defense to keep the ball out of the middle area as much as possible? Diagram 3-10 illustrates the offensive passing options when the ball is in the middle of the court. The spread offensive set shown emphasizes the offensive advantage that the ball handler, 1, has, in as much as all four of his teammates are potential pass receivers. This kind of offensive situation restricts the deployment of the defensive players, particularly when the defense is applying pressure tactics. Notice in Diagram 3-11 the improvement in the defensive situation that is brought about when the ball is passed out of the middle. The same improvement would be gained by forcing 1 to dribble the ball out of the middle. X3 and X4 are relieved of the

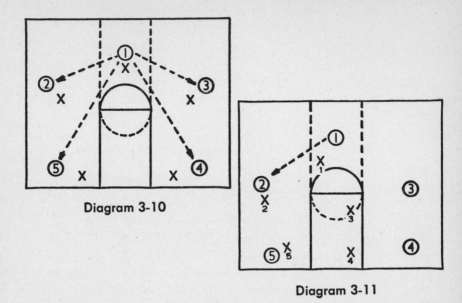

Diagram 3-10

Diagram 3-11

responsibility of covering a potential pass receiver, and they can adjust their position in such a way that they are providing security for the basket. 3 is two passes removed from the ball, and 4 is three passes removed from the ball. The basic offensive concept involves being able to pass the ball in either direction from the middle of the court. Conversely, the defense wants to limit the direction of the pass by forcing the ball out of the middle.

An offensive player dribbling the basketball in the middle should be forced to dribble out of this area. Once the dribbler is out of the middle, the defensive player must make certain that the dribbler does not "turn the corner" on him and beat him down the sideline or on the baseline. The coach will apparently be giving contradictory instructions when he says, "force him out of the middle" on the one hand, and "get outside" on the other. The decision to pressure all penetrating passes requires that the man guarding the dribbler take care of the sideline and the baseline. The deep defensive player cannot pressure the receiver and provide help on the dribbler. The help is in the middle of the court, and if the dribbler continues to keep his dribble alive, eventually he will be forced back to help in the middle. In Diagram 3-12, X1 forces 1 out of the middle and then must get outside 1 to prevent the drive to the basket. X2 cannot pressure the potential pass

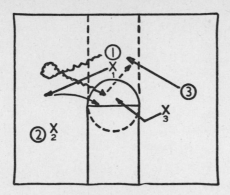

Diagram 3-12

receiver, 2, and also be expected to provide help for X1 on the sideline. The decision to pressure passes toward the basket overrides the defensive efforts to keep the ball out of the middle. X1 gets outside and forces the dribbler toward his teammates even at the expense of the ball returning to the middle area. X3 in the diagram provides the front line support. This help by X3 leaves 3 open for a pass into the middle. However, this pass from 1 to 3 is away from the basket and is to be preferred to the drive down the middle of the defense that would occur if X3 did not help X1.

Diagram 3-13 illustrates the defensive position of each man when the ball is on the side of the court. Defensive men X5 and X3 are on the ball side of their men, discouraging the pass into the middle area. X4 is pressuring the possible penetrating pass to 4. When the dribbler is

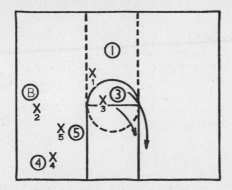

Diagram 3-13

dead, X1 can move out into an area between 1 and the ball and play the passing lane. As long as the ball handler has his dribble coming, X1 is the first line of support and should help X2 as he forces 2 to dribble to the middle.

Diagram 3-14 illustrates the probable offensive counter to the defensive adjustments described above. 2 dribbles to the middle, and X1, who is playing as deep as the ball, helps on the dribbler, 2. 2 passes to 1 in the middle area. Again, the defense is permitting the ball to go into the middle area, but this is to be preferred to the drive down the lane by 2. Remember too, that the pass from 2 to 1 is away from the basket. Now, with the ball in the middle in 1's possession, the entire series of events begins all over. X1 gets back to his man, forces him out of the middle, then gets outside to keep him from driving the sideline, and so on.

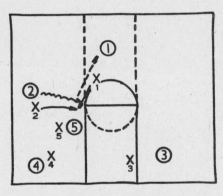

Diagram 3-14

Defensive Position and Adjustment on the Movement of the Ball

The position of the defensive man guarding the ball has been described in detail in Chapter 2. Those defensive players covering a potential pass receiver who is nearer to the basket than to the ball use the three-quarter position, which is also described in Chapter 2. The defensive position presently under consideration deals primarily with those players at least two passes removed from the ball. In Diagram 3-15, 2 has the basketball, and the defensive position of X4 is that described previously as defensing the strong side forward. X1 covers

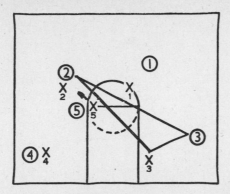

Diagram 3-15

his man in accordance with the techniques for defensing the offside guard. X5 follows the principles of defensive post play. In order to determine his correct defensive position, X3 draws an imaginary line between his man, 3, and the ball. X3 then backs off that line into a position from which he can see both his man and the ball. In order to insure that X3's position is open, he can be instructed to point at his man with his right hand and at the ball with his left hand. X3 should face a point midway between the ball and 3 such that both are within the span of his peripheral vision. When X3 backs off the imaginary line between the ball and his man, he must bear two things in mind: (1) back up far enough so that he can see both his man and the ball and (2) the farther the man is from the ball, the farther he should be from his man.

Two things can happen that would cause X3 to have to adjust his position. The first of these is that the position of the ball changes. Diagrams 3-16 and 3-17 illustrate the defensive adjustment X3 should make on movement of the ball.

In Diagram 3-16, 2 passes to 4. Now X3 is three passes removed from the ball and thus drops off his man even farther. Note also that 1 is now two passes away from the ball, and that X1 has dropped farther off him into the middle.

In Diagram 3-17, 2 passes to 1. Note the defensive adjustments of X3 and X4. X3 is now covering a man who is one penetrating pass away from the ball. X3 is defensing the strong side forward and must assume the three-quarter defensive position on 3. X4 is now covering a man two passes removed from the ball and determines his position by backing off the imaginary line between 4 and the ball.

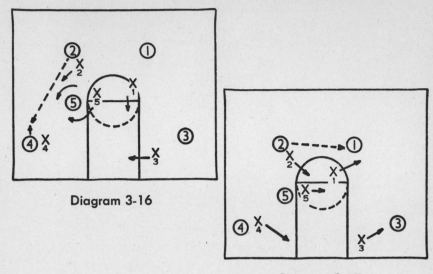

Diagram 3-16

Diagram 3-17

The second thing which would cause X3 to adjust his position would be for his assigned man, 3, to move. Diagram 3-18 illustrates 3 moving toward the baseline. The imaginary line between the ball and 3 now places X3 directly on that line. From this position X3 can see either the ball or the man, but not both. X3 must adjust his position by backing off this line until both the ball and the man come into his field of vision.

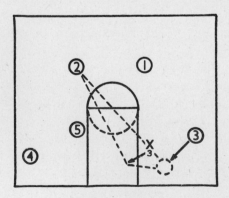

Diagram 3-18

Diagram 3-19 offers an example of movement by 3 which would place him one penetrating pass away from the ball. X3 now must adjust his position accordingly by playing a three-quarter position on 3.

Each time the ball moves, all five defensive players must adjust their positions. Each time an offensive player moves, the defensive man assigned to guard him must adjust his position.

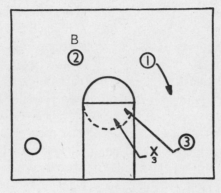

Diagram 3-19

Double-Team Opportunities

Within the confines of sound defensive philosophy there will be times when the ball handler can be two-timed, doubled-teamed or trapped, depending upon which term you prefer. The risk involved in any unusual defensive tactic must be measured in terms of the percentages. What does the defense stand to gain by resorting to such tactics as compared with the possibility of making defensive mistakes that would be costly? Does the advantage of success outweigh the dangers involved in failure? What percentage of the time will the special tactic succeed and what will be the probable results when the tactic fails? Before deciding when to utilize the double-team technique, the above questions must be answered satisfactorily.

The double-team technique can safely be used as a basic defensive tool in specific situations. When the offensive man with the ball turns his back to the basket, he not only is unable to see his teammates, but he is also unaware of the positions of the defensive players on the court. If you are guarding a player in the proximity of the ball handler, and the ball handler turns his back to the basket, only a calculated risk is involved in leaving your assigned man to double-team the ball. The ball handler will almost invariably pass the basketball in the direction he is facing. An excellent opportunity to double-team occurs when your assigned opponent takes you near the ball, and the player with the ball has his back to you. This situation can occur when the defensive man is applying a lot of pressure on the ball handler and is forcing him to pivot in order to protect the ball. This situation also occurs frequently when the dribbler executes a reverse dribble. The reverse dribble, which involves a 360° pivot, is a dangerous offensive move in a crowded area.

In the basic man-for-man defense each defender should be as deep as the ball. When your assigned offensive player is behind the line of the ball, and you are as deep as the ball, you can afford to double-team on the ball. In order for the ball to be passed to your man, it must be passed away from the basket. A defensive player who retreats quickly after losing possession of the ball will have this opportunity to double-team. A similar opportunity occurs when the offensive player has possession of the ball in the basket area. In this situation the defensive player or players nearest the ball should double-team or gang the ball handler.

Each of the situations described are considered calculated risks and a part of the basic man-for-man defense. The defensive stance of the two players doubling up on the ball handler should be erect with their hands up above their head. The position of the defenders should be very close to the ball handler. The man involved in the trap should try to steal the ball if the offensive player fails to protect it. The defensive players must be careful about reaching for the ball and committing a foolish foul. When a defensive man plays the ball, he must move his body into a position from which he can reach the ball while his hands are in front of him and close to his body. He should not reach around the offensive player for the ball, but rather, should move his body so that the ball is in front of him. Extending the arms will cause the offensive man to throw a high pass over the defensive man's hands or to use a bounce pass to get the ball out of the trap. Either of these passes will give the trapper's teammates a good opportunity to intercept. The defensive man should be alert to tie the ball up and force a jump ball.

Once the trap is established and the players are committed to it, they must keep the pressure on the ball handler. It is their responsibility to prevent the ball handler from making a good pass. If the ball handler is alive and tries to dribble out of the trap, the defenders must come shoulder to shoulder and prevent the dribbler from splitting them. Diagram 3-20 illustrates the duties of the defenders against a dribbler.

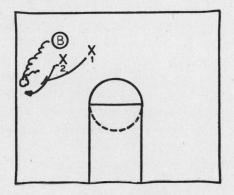

Diagram 3-20

X1 and X2 must play close enough to each other so that the ball handler cannot dribble between them. Should the dribbler start down the sideline, X2 must get outside the dribbler and force him to stop or reverse his dribble. X1 trails the dribble and, when B reverses his dribble, X1 must move in close to X2 and prevent B from splitting them. If B continues to dribble as shown in Diagram 3-21, X1 must prevent him from getting the opposite sideline advantage, and X2 will trail and is responsible for stopping the drive between the two defen-

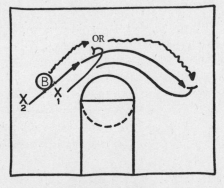

Diagram 3-21

ders. The situation shown in the diagrams is a very good drill in which to practice the double-team techniques.

The situations just mentioned are calculated risks and are considered a part of the basic man-for-man defense. There are other opportunities to double-team, which involve greater risk, and which are used as variations of the basic defense and in special situations.

Trapping in the corner is a variation of the basic defense which can be used in special situations as described in Chapter 10. Special options exist when the opponents are taking the ball out of bounds after a field goal or free throw has been scored. The variations that the defender covering the offensive player making the throw-in has at his disposal include double-teaming opportunities. For example, he may elect not to cover the throw-in man, but to double-team a particular inbounds opponent in an effort to force the pass to another offensive player. He could elect to play back off of the man making the throw-in and double-team after the inbounds pass has been completed. In special defenses, such as the catch-up defense, the defensive players should be alert for opportunities to double-team the ball. Such opportunities would exist: when the opponents screen on the point of the ball; when a teammate off the ball has to help on a drive (he can stay with the driver and effect a double-team); in a desperation situation (any time your man takes you close enough to the ball). The double-team opportunities that are not a part of the basic defense, but are variations of the basic defense, are covered extensively in Chapter 10.

4

Organizing the Man-for-Man Defense

Many teams are capable of playing a very tough defense once they are all set up and ready to play. A big part of defensive organization involves getting from the offensive end of the court back to the predetermined point of attack. The transition from offense to defense must be made quickly and with a thorough understanding of the team defense being employed.

Much has been said and written about the fast break as an offensive weapon. The defensive break is even more important. The increased emphasis being placed on the fast-break offense with its sophisticated trailer action makes defensive organization a more vital phase of the overall defensive plan. Many modern offenses are designed to produce a scoring opportunity after one or two passes. The quick-shot offense makes it imperative that the defense not only retreat hurriedly to the defensive end of the court, but that they also move as quickly as possible into the proper defensive position on their assigned man.

Court Balance

The most frequent way the offense loses the ball is that which occurs when the defense recovers the rebound from a missed shot.

In order for the offensive team to make the transition to defense in an organized manner, specific offensive principles must be adhered to. The offensive style of play must be one which provides court balance. Court balance refers to the positions on the court of the five offensive players when the shot is taken. The responsibilities of the players, when their team shoots the ball, will vary depending upon the emphasis the opponent places on the fast break. The responsibilities of the offensive players will also vary in accordance with the particular offensive set being used. The abilities of the individual players will influence their assignments when the shot is taken.

Ideally, the position of the offensive player on the court at the time the shot is taken should determine his responsibility. Specific plays that produce scoring opportunities insure that certain players are in rebounding position when the shot is taken. These plays further insure that players are located in a safety position from which they can retreat quickly and protect the basket.

Each team must have an organized plan that insures court balance. In order to place responsibilities and to simplify the procedure, the individuals in the offense are assigned a specific duty each time a shot is taken. The guards have the safety responsibility and are expected to be the first men back on defense to protect against the long pass, etc. The center and the forwards, because of their positions in the offense and their size, are expected to hit the boards, and they have the rebounding duties.

Obviously, the designation of specified players to rebound and others to "bounce out" and balance the court will not provide the best court balance in every situation that occurs. Many times the guard may be caught inside when the shot is taken, and the forward may be too far from the basket to get to the boards to rebound. However, the placement of individual responsibility, and the removal of indecision as to what to do outweigh the disadvantage of occassionally being caught out of position.

Like any other rule, there will be exceptions. The one time the guard is relieved of his safety responsibilities is when he drives to the basket. The offense should be designed in such a way that one guard is always back or moving in that direction. The guard, who is not back as safety, is designated as the half-and-half man and should move into the area of the free throw line when the shot is taken. The other three big men should move into the basket area for rebounding purposes.

Diagram 4-1 illustrates the position of the offense when the shot is taken. 1 is the safety and 2 is designated as half rebounder and half safety. 2 is responsible for the long rebound in the free throw area. 2 also reacts to long rebounds in the corners. If the ball rebounds in a direction away from him, he immediately begins retreating to help 1 as safety.

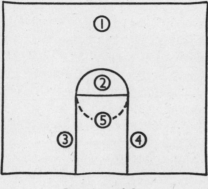

Diagram 4-1

The number of offensive players that are sent to the boards depends upon the threat of the fast break that is presented by the opponents. Four, or even five men can be designated as offensive rebounders when the opponent refuses to throw the long pass or to utilize the fast break. Diagram 4-2 illustrates the offensive team balancing the court after a shot with both guards on the free throw line. This forma-

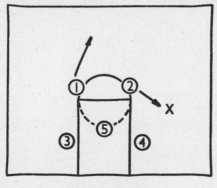

Diagram 4-2

tion is not as dangerous as it appears when 1 and 2 coordinate their efforts. 1 and 2 have the responsibility for the long rebounds. The ball rebounds long into the area designated by the X in Diagram 4-2. 2 reacts to the direction of the rebound, and 1 must retreat immediately since the ball rebounds away from him. Proper court balance is essential to orderly defensive organization.

In an effort to continue to follow the principle of simplicity, the court balance responsibility is designated according to a player's position—e.g. guard, forward or center. One additional rule is added which applies to all five players: Each time the shot is taken, you must do one of two things—(1) hit the boards or (2) bounce out. Each player is expected to use good judgment in deciding which of these two things he will do. There will be times, perhaps, when all of the players decide to bounce out. The opponent's fast break will certainly be stymied when all of the offensive players retreat quickly to the defensive goal. On other occasions all of the players may decide to rebound. Five offensive players, hitting the boards aggressively, offer an excellent chance to capture the rebound. The important point is that each player must do one of these two things on every shot. The times a team gets burned is when one or more players stand around after the shot and fail to follow or to bounce out. These players who stand around are referred to as "spectators" and should be informed that they should have to buy a ticket to watch the game.

The Defensive Break

The defensive break refers to the quickness with which a team makes the transition from offense to defense. The instant possession of the ball is lost, the team becomes a defensive team. Some opponents present offensive threats of such magnitude that a team must become a defensive team as soon as it becomes apparent that they will lose possession of the basketball. This anticipation provides the defense with a few additional seconds in which to retreat and pick up their men. Good floor balance is essential to the proper execution of the defensive break.

The guards are designated to be the first two players back on defense when the ball is rebounded by the opponents. These two players must learn to protect for one another. The guards should never be caught under the basket at the same time when a shot comes as the result of the set offense. The third man back on defense is determined by the direction in which the shot rebounds. In Diagram 4-3 the ball rebounds in the area between 5 and 3. Since the ball rebounds in their direction, 5 and 3 are reacting to the ball. The ball rebounds away from 4, and since it is impossible for him to get the rebound, he should start for the defensive end of the court. Assume that 5 gets the offensive rebound. 5 can hold up and wait for his teammates, 1, 2, and 4 to get back into offensive formation and set up another scoring opportunity.

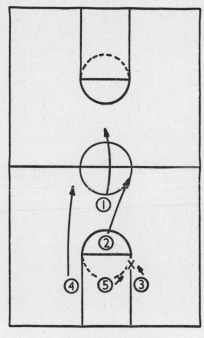

Diagram 4-3

If the defense recovers the rebound, and they usually will, then 4 is well on his way to provide defensive help for the guards, 1 and 2. The quickness with which the offside rebounder reacts to the direction of the rebound is instrumental in the development of the defensive break. This player is the key man in preventing the defense from getting outnumbered by the offensive fast break.

The two guards and the deep man opposite the rebound are the first three players back on defense. The remaining two players are usually in the vicinity of the basketball when the defense gets the rebound. In special situations one or both of these players can apply pressure to the rebounder to prevent or slow down the outlet pass. These players must sprint to the defensive end of the court as quickly as possible in order to carry out their defensive rebounding duties. In Diagram 4-4, 5 and 3 have reacted to the rebound, which is gathered in by X5. 4 must release and sprint to the defensive end of the court. As 4 retreats, he must locate his assigned man, X4. As he nears his man, he should point at him and shout to his teammates, "I've got X4." This communication by 4 relieves 1 and 2 of the concern about X4 and permits them to concentrate on making certain that the other offensive players are covered. 2 is responsible for making certain that an opponent does not get behind him. 2 covers the first man down the court and continues to check him until his assigned man picks him up. As the safety, 2 can retreat by running backwards, keeping the other nine players, and the ball, in front of him. Running backwards gives 2 a good view of the entire situation. This view enables him not only to pick up the first man down the court, but it also aids him in giving instructions to his teammates, relative to who needs to be covered, etc.

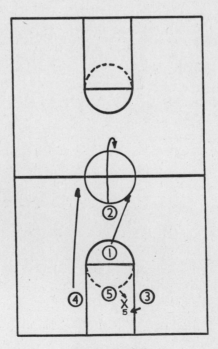

Diagram 4-4

The offense is able to get a cheap basket as a result of a long pass up the court against teams that do not know where the ball is as they go back on defense. As the players run toward their man to get in the proper defensive position, they should be looking over their shoulder toward the basketball. When the position of the ball is changed, the player retreating should pivot in such a way that he opens up to the ball. In order to pick off or deflect the long pass, the defender must be able to see the ball. The problem of protecting against the long pass is comparable to that of a defensive halfback in football. A drill used early in the season to practice on this footwork is called the defensive halfback drill, and is shown in Diagram 4-5. The coach or manager has the ball as shown by B. Five players at a time are lined up across the court with instructions to sprint to the opposite end of the court. Each player is facing the direction of the arrow because the ball is on that side of the court. Upon receiving the instruction "go," the players run, looking over their left shoulder at the ball as they sprint toward the opposite end of the court. The ball is passed across the baseline as shown, and now the players are to find the ball by looking over their right shoulder. Emphasis is placed on the technique used in changing from the former position to the latter one. Each player must pivot in such a way that he opens up toward the ball, keeping it constantly in his view. The diagram illustrates the ball being returned to the original position with the second pivot by the players. The footwork used in this drill is very similar to that described earlier as the reverse-retreat step, except that here it is performed at full speed. Again, the defense, as it retreats, should not turn its back on the ball.

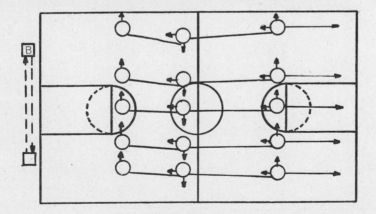

Diagram 4-5

Picking Up Your Assigned Man

Many teams hustle to the defensive end of the court upon losing possession of the ball. Normally, the team is instructed to retreat to the basket, then find their man and move out into the regular defensive position. A major part of defensive organization involves the techniques used in moving from the basket area into the proper defensive position on your assigned man. The quickness with which the defense becomes properly positioned will determine the opportunity available for the offense to take advantage of a defensive lapse.

The offensive team that dribbles the ball up the court slowly allows the opposition adequate time to set its defense in its predetermined pick-up positions. Against such teams the defense can hustle back into their defense and wait for the offense to come to them. These types of offensive teams pose few problems as far as defensive organization is concerned. Most teams, however, are not so accommodating.

The first man back will have to check a teammate's assigned man on many occassions. In Diagram 4-6, 4 is covered initially by X2. X2

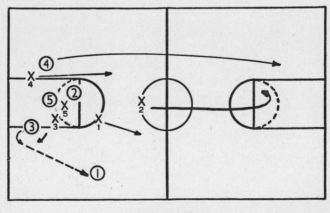

Diagram 4-6

must stay with 4 until the proper situation arises for him to pick up his assigned man, 2. Each player should point to the man he is covering as he falls back on defense. Each player should also communicate to his teammates the number of the player he is covering. Not only should the defensive team talk, but they should listen for instructions from teammates in key positions as well. Many defensive mistakes can be prevented through communication. An alert defense can recover from mistakes that have been committed before the offense takes advantage of the mistake.

Diagram 4-7 points out a situation in which X2 is required to stay with 4. X2 and X4 must pick the proper time to switch back to their assigned men. X2 should not leave 4 as long as 4 is under the basket. The defensive man farthest from the basket releases and goes inside to his original man. Only then can the inside man move out to pick up his assigned man. 1 passes the ball to 3. With the ball on the opposite side of the court, the offense has given X4 an ideal situation in which to move under the basket and pick up 4. After X4 is in position, X2 will move out to 2. If an offensive player must be left unguarded momentarily, make certain that it is an outside player.

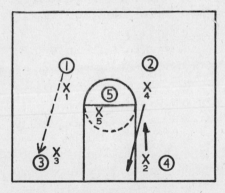

Diagram 4-7

The problem of picking up his assigned man is not difficult for the player assigned to cover the rebounder. In the vast majority of cases, the rebounder will be the last man down the court. The player assigned to cover the rebounder can position himself in such a way that he can provide help for his teammates by quickly retreating to the line of the ball. Diagram 4-8 illustrates X5 quickly getting as deep as the ball. All five defensive players should make every effort to stay up with the ball as it moves up the court. The defense has done a good job when the offense is forced to pass the ball backwards.

Scoring a field goal provides a situation that affords the defense adequate time to hustle back and pick up their assigned men. If a team

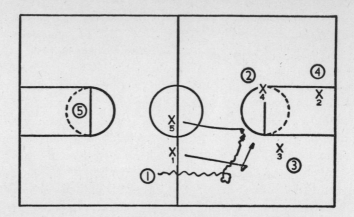

Diagram 4-8

can take the ball out-of-bounds after the goal is scored, and then beat the defense to the other end, the defense is very poor and is just plain loafing.

Out-of-bounds situations, other than after a goal, provide even more time for the defense to set up since the rules require that the official handle the ball.

There are some situations that can not be defensed. These situations originate with offensive errors. There is no way that a defense can recover quickly enough to prevent a layup when a cross-court pass is intercepted. Even after an interception the shooter may miss the basket, so all players must constantly be reminded that "you are never too late on defense." The defense should hustle back and recover the rebound, thus eliminating the second shot. A team's offensive play affects its defense in several ways. The offense has opportunities to limit the opponent's scoring by: (1) maintaining good court balance, (2) reducing offensive errors such as bad passes and fumbles, (3) taking only good shots, and (4) tough offensive rebounding.

Defense is usually practiced on a half-court situation, with the defense in position when the ball is handed to the offensive team. However, basketball is becoming more of a full-court game, with the advent of various full-court defenses and fast-break offenses. Most coaches spend too little time using the entire court in practice. It is not realistic to practice defense solely on half of the court. The defensive break and defensive organization cannot be taught or practiced on part

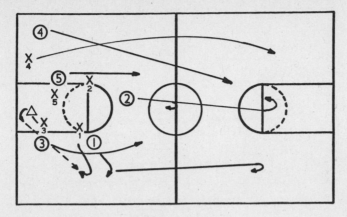

Diagram 4-9

of the court. A method used to practice the complete sequence and scope of defense is shown in Diagram 4-9. The team represented by the O's in the diagram are on offense. Such offensive points as court balance, shot selection, taking care of the ball, and offensive rebounding can be emphasized. When the defense gains possession of the ball as a result of a defensive rebound, interception, or out-of-bounds situation, the X's revert to offense, and the offensive team is placed in a game-like situation in which they must make a quick transition from offense to defense with all of the corresponding communication and teamwork involved in picking up their assigned men, etc. Variations of the defense, such as the 50 or 75 defense, must be rehearsed in this manner, too. The organization involved in picking up assigned players is one of the most difficult defensive tasks to master.

Stopping the Fast Break

The particular type of fast break a team employs will influence the choice of defensive tactics used to stop their break. In addition to the offensive measures that can aid the defense, there are several specific defensive steps that can be taken to slow down the fast-breaking team.

Diagram 4-10 illustrates a basic fast-break pattern which is widely used. Teams that run other patterns are usually similar to, or a variation of, this basic pattern. Regardless of the particular pattern used, the ingredients that are essential for a successful fast break are identical.

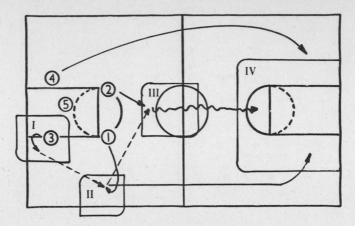

Diagram 4-10

Analyzing the offensive components of the fast break will indicate the specific areas in which it can be defensed.

The areas squared in the diagram illustrate the phases of the development of the fast break. The square marked "I" shows the fast break beginning when 3 gets the rebound. In order for a team to employ the fast break successfully, it must be able to control the defensive boards. It logically follows that strong, aggressive, offensive rebounding would be one way to counter the fast break. When the offense sends four, four and a half, or five men to the boards, they greatly increase their chances of getting an offensive rebound. 1 and 2 in the diagram frequently anticipate the recovery of a missed shot by their teammates and take off early. Diagram 4-11 illustrates the advantage the offense has on the board when 1 and 2 move out before their teammates have actually rebounded the missed shot.

Quite obviously, this offensive maneuver presents a calculated risk. Should the defense control the rebound and clear the ball from the basket area, they will have an advantage in numbers at the other end. The decision to send extra men to the offensive boards must be made by weighing the number of offensive rebounds recovered against the number of easy baskets given up as a result of this tactic.

In order for a team to be effective with the fast break, it must not only control the defensive boards, but the rebounder must be able to make the outlet pass quickly and accurately. Making the outlet pass requires a great deal of skill and is a difficult task under normal condi-

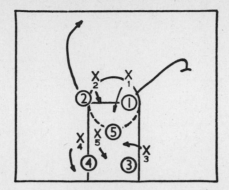

Diagram 4-11

tions. The defense can make this task even more difficult by applying pressure to the rebounder the instant he gains control of the rebound.

Diagram 4-12 illustrates X3 anticipating the rebounder 3 pivoting toward the baseline as he looks for the outlet pass receiver. 3 will normally use a one-hand baseball pass or a hook pass in this situation.

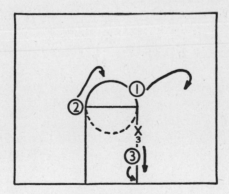

Diagram 4-12

X3 should overplay the passing hand with both arms extended high above his head. When X3 can cause 3 to delay the outlet pass, he has done a good job of pressuring the rebounder. If 3 is forced to look for a secondary receiver or to dribble the ball toward the corner in order to clear the basket area, X3 has provided enough pressure to give his teammates time to get back into defensive position.

Defensive strategy could warrant pressuring the rebounder with two men. Diagram 4-13 illustrates X3 applying baseline pressure to the rebounder 3, and X5 doubling from the front.

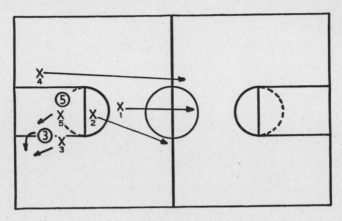

Diagram 4-13

When the defense rebounds the ball in the middle of the court, the player applying pressure must play more squarely. The rebounder who gets the ball in front of the basket will usually pivot in such a way that he can make the outlet pass with his dominant hand. Diagram 4-14 illustrates 5, who is right-handed, rebounding the ball and turning so that he can use his right hand to make the outlet pass. X5, in pressuring the rebounder, should favor the dominant hand of the rebounder.

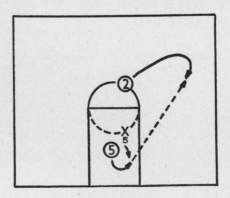

Diagram 4-14

The second area in which the defense can make a concerted effort to contain the fast break is marked II in Diagram 4-10. The basketball must be cleared quickly from the congested basket area in order to initiate the break. The defensive team, as it retreats, normally retreats in straight lines down the middle of the court. Consequently, the rebounder looks first to the sideline for an outlet pass.

Many fast-breaking teams have a favorite receiver for the outlet pass. This receiver is their best ball handler, who, upon receiving the outlet pass, immediately takes the ball to the middle with a dribble. This key player is expected to get a good shot or make an assist on the scoring end of the break. When a team has a ball handler upon which the success of the fast break depends, the defense can overplay this man in an effort to keep him from receiving the outlet pass. Diagram 4-15 illustrates X1 reacting to the outlet pass receiver in an effort to intercept the pass. When X1 cuts off the passing lane to 1, he can force the rebounder to make the outlet pass to a receiver of his second choice.

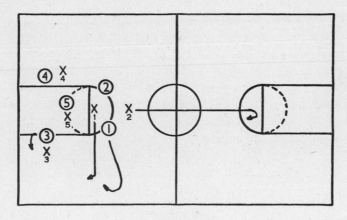

Diagram 4-15

X1, as he moves toward the sideline to play the outlet pass to 1, must use good judgment in attempting the interception. X1 should play the ball if his chances of success are favorable. When the opportunity to intercept involves a gamble, X1 should play position on 1. Diagram 4-16 illustrates the route of X1 as he retreats into defensive position on 1. From this position X1 should be alert for the opportunity to draw the

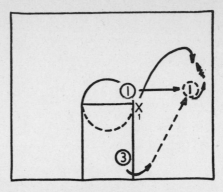

Diagram 4-16

charging foul from 1. Many times 1 will receive the outlet pass, pivot toward the sideline and automatically put the ball on the floor. If 1 fails to come under control, turn, and look up court prior to beginning his dribble, he will be susceptible to charging the defensive man.

The opportunity to draw the foul will not be present against a sound ball handler. In any event, X1 can apply pressure to 1 and do everything within his power to delay his progress.

The third area in which the fast break can be defensed (marked III in Diagram 4-10) is in the mid-court area. The second pass in the fast break is from the outlet receiver to an offside teammate cutting toward the mid-court area. This pass is illustrated in Diagram 4-10 when 1 passes to 2. If the defensive plan involves applying pressure in the middle area, X2 in Diagram 4-17 does not retreat quickly, but rather

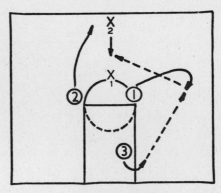

Diagram 4-17

contests 2 for the pass into the middle. X2 must play the ball or play position. When the pass is completed from 1 to 2, X2 may have an opportunity to draw the charging foul. X2 should apply pressure on 2 when he receives the ball, and do all he can to delay 2's effort to dribble the ball into the scoring area. When X2 can slow 2's dribble, he provides his teammates with an opportunity to come up behind 2 and deflect his dribble, as shown in Diagram 4-18. Defensive players X4 and X1, as they retreat to the line of the ball, have the opportunity to play 2's dribble from behind.

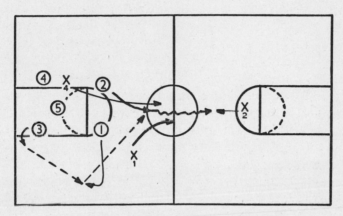

Diagram 4-18

Area IV in Diagram 4-10 represents the scoring area for the fast-break team. All defensive players should be prepared to cope with situations in this area where the offense has the defense outnumbered. These disadvantage situations usually take the form of a two-on-one, three-on-one, or a three-on-two.

When faced with a two-on-one situation, the lone defender should retreat quickly to the basket area. The defensive player's primary concern should be to prevent the layup. In this situation the defensive man should fake, bluff, and yell in his effort to slow down the offensive players. If the defender can delay the attack, even slightly, or force a jump shot or even cause the offense to make an extra pass in their attempt to score, he has done well. Ideally, the defensive man should fake an attack at the dribbler and cause him to pick up his dribble. The defensive player should retreat under the basket and check the second man in the attack. The defender should avoid running off the court as the offensive players drive to the basket. In the event the shot is missed, he should be prepared to get the rebound.

The offense, with a two-on-one advantage, should score a driving layup. Because of this reality, the defender is permitted more leeway in gambling when confronted with this situation. For example, if the two attacking offensive players are passing the ball back and forth as they move toward their goal, the defensive man is free to attempt an interception.

The defender's best chance, when confronted with a three against one situation, is to try to draw the charging foul. The middle man on the attack usually has the ball as the three offensive players move down the court. If the defensive man attacks the dribbler, he will force the dribbler to pass the ball to one of his teammates. The middle man frequently does not have his body under control, and continues his movement forward after he passes off. The defender can position himself in the path of the middle man and draw the charging foul. This action by the defensive man, when successful, is one of the biggest defensive plays that can be made. The layup, coming after the pass, is nullified, and the defender's team gains possession of the basketball. Additionally, one of the opponent's key players has picked up an additional foul.

A three against two is a situation in which any two team members may find themselves. The two defensive players must retreat quickly to the scoring area and locate themselves in a tandem formation, with one player in front of the basket, and the other near the head of the circle. As the two defenders retreat, they must communicate with each other in order to insure that one will cover the ball, and the other the hole or basket area. The only practical application of defense in an outnumbered situation is for the defense to play a zone. The two defenders play a two-man zone with one player guarding the ball, and the other player guarding the basket, as shown in Diagram 4-19.

When the ball is passed out of the middle, the zone assignments are switched. X2 moves out to cover the first pass, and X1 retreats to cover the basket, as shown in Diagram 4-20. As X1 retreats to the basket area, he should pivot in such a way that he is opened up to the ball. The offense will be unable to pass the ball to a receiver under the basket if the defense reacts properly and quickly. The only pass that is available is for the wing man to pass the ball back to the middle as shown in Diagram 4-21. As the ball goes back to the middle, the

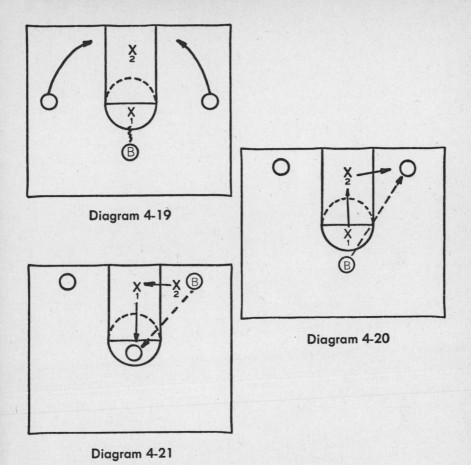

Diagram 4-19

Diagram 4-20

Diagram 4-21

defenders slide back to their original positions. When the defense forces the offense to make several passes, the defenders have provided time for their teammates to retreat and neutralize the offensive advantage.

A drill designed to improve the defensive break is shown in Diagram 4-22. Three offensive players (O's) are stationed out-of-bounds at the end of the court in fast-break fashion. The defensive player in front of the offensive player receiving the ball must touch the baseline before he can retreat on defense. The other two defensive players must defend against three offensive players until their teammate arrives. The coach passes the ball to 2. 2, 3, and 1 attack defenders X1 and X3. X2 must touch the baseline, then hustle back to pick up his man. X1 and

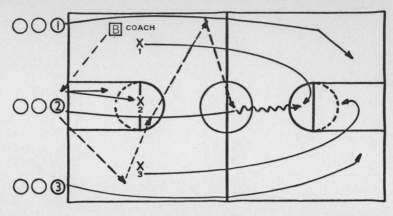

Diagram 4-22

X3 must communicate while getting lined up in a tandem zone. This drill presents a game-like situation in as much as X1 and X3 must employ delaying tactics until X2 gets back to pick up his man.

The particular point or points that the defense wants to attack in its effort to stop the fast break depends on a number of factors. An excellent rule which would always be applicable in stopping the fast break would be, "Apply pressure to the ball continuously until the defense is back and organized." Each team member should be aware of the various points of attack in stopping the fast break. The action taken by an individual will depend upon his location on the court at the time the shot is taken. If he is playing the rebound and the opponents get possession, he would be in a good position to apply pressure to the rebounder. If a defensive player found himself on the sideline or in the middle of the court when the opponents gain possession of the rebound, he should apply pressure in the appropriate area. Any time the defense can "stop the dribbler," they have delayed the attack and provided more time for the defense to retreat and get organized.

5

How to Cover the Post with the Man-for-Man

There are many considerations that must be taken into account when planning a post defense. The position in which the post sets up, whether he moves continuously, his particular strengths and weaknesses, the strengths and weaknesses of the other players on his team, and the basic formation the offense is using are some of the factors that must be taken into consideration when faced with the problem of defensing the post.

The terms *post*, *post man*, *center*, *pivot*, *pivot man*, etc. are frequently used interchangeably. Some coaches define each of these words in terms of the duties of a particular player. Technically, the latter definition is correct, but the term *post* or *post man* will be used hereafter to mean a player who usually sets up in the proximity of the basket, with back toward the goal. He may be stationed thusly in order to: (1) receive the ball and score, (2) receive the ball and pass off to cutting teammates, (3) set screens for his teammates, and (4) be in a favorable rebounding position when a teammate shoots the ball.

Guidelines for Defensive Post Play

In spite of the many and varied factors involved in developing a defense that will effectively neutralize offensive post play, the coach must have a place to begin. Most teams that utilize post play do so because the man inside their offense is an able scorer or because the offensive patterns and plays are designed to revolve around him. In either of the cases the objectives of the defense will counter these offensive aims. Two of the defensive objectives are: (1) to stop the close shots, and (2) to force the offense out of its basic pattern.

The basic approach to defensive post play is predicated upon these two factors: (1) the position of the post man, and (2) the location of the basketball. From here certain principles of defensive position can be established. Diagram 5-1 illustrates the normal positions in which the offensive post man will set up. These positions are classified as low (L), medium (M), or high (H) post position. All of these positions are inside the area of the court considered the scoring area. In accordance with the basic rules governing a player inside this area, as well as the rule concerning a penetrating pass, the defensive post man must apply pressure to the receiver and make him move to get open. Generally, any player in the low post position must be fronted. A post man in the medium post position will be played with the three-quarter defensive position previously described in regard to defensing the strong side forward. The defensive post man will normally play beside a high post man, on the ball side, in what is referred to as the one-half defensive position.

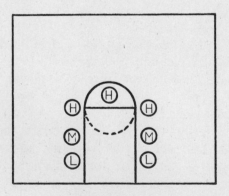

Diagram 5-1

The location of the basketball on the court aids the defensive post man in determining which side of the offensive man he should play. The defensive post man must determine the location of the ball with respect to the imaginary line shown in Diagram 5-2.

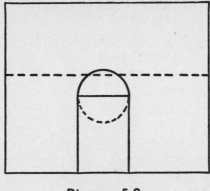

Diagram 5-2

When the ball is outside the line, as shown in Diagram 5-3, the defensive post man favors the inside or lane side of his man.

With the ball on the baseline side of the imaginary line, the post man favors the baseline side of the offensive player as shown in Diagram 5-4.

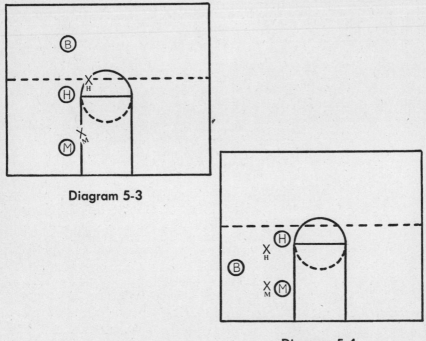

Diagram 5-3

Diagram 5-4

Defensing the Moving Post

Many teams that feature an agile offensive player with good height and great one-on-one moves near the basket design their team offense in such a way that the area near the basket belongs to the offensive post man. The other four team members are often relegated to supporting cast and are practically forbidden to enter the sacred area near the basket for fear that it will crowd things up for the post man. Diagram 5-5 illustrates the area to be kept open for the post and some of the offensive moves he might make in order to get open to receive a pass. The four perimeter players have the responsibility of moving the ball while they are constantly looking for an opportunity to pass to the post. The post may run a figure of eight in an effort to get open for a pass. The post man will usually front the ball as it moves around the outside, using a series of quick stops and starts, change of directions, and change of pace in an effort to free himself for a pass.

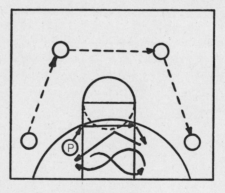

Diagram 5-5

The post man who has so much freedom is difficult to cover. The defensive post man must depend on his teammates and the team defense to provide help for him when he is confronted with this situation. To the best of his ability the defensive post man should attempt to gain the defensive position based on the position of the post man and the location of the ball as previously explained. The defensive post man must understand that it is impossible to prevent the ball from getting into the offensive player all of the time. He must do his very best to make it difficult for the ball to go inside. In order to minimize the number of times the post receives the ball, the defensive post man must *move on each pass*. He cannot wait until the offensive player makes a move toward the ball and then react. If he does this the offensive player will position him and be open to receive the pass. The defender would be wise to think like an offensive post man and anticipate the spots the offensive player will move to—and beat him to these spots. The defensive post man must not be afraid of being caught in front of the offensive post man occasionally; he must have confidence in his teammates and their ability to help out on the lob pass.

Beating the offensive player to the spot sets up a change of direction cut for the offensive post. Diagram 5-6 illustrates the basic offensive move used to combat the fronting defense. X5 in the diagram should be moving toward the ball, ahead of 5, in a closed position with his left foot forward and his left hand extended. When 5 makes his change of direction, X5 opens to the ball, pivots on his right foot and swings his left foot around toward the baseline. X5 from this position may have to take a quick hop toward 5 in order to regain the normal guarding distance. The defensive footwork used when the offensive player changes directions is shown in Diagram 5-7. X5 should avoid getting locked in a fronting position with his tail to 5. This position is one from which X5 cannot see 5, and it affords 5 opportunities to break into open passing lanes or retreat to the basket without X5's knowledge. In those instances where X5 must move across in front of 5, X5 should feel 5 during the momentary span of time during which X5 cannot see 5. When X5 cannot feel 5, he must quickly retreat and adjust his position in such a way that 5 returns to his field of vision.

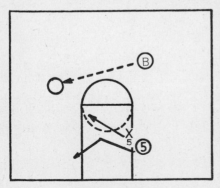

Diagram 5-6

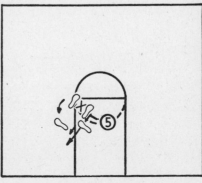

Diagram 5-7

Five offensive players against one defensive post man is an excellent defensive post drill. The four players on the perimeter pass the ball around the outside looking for an opportunity to hit the post as the offensive post man moves to get open for the pass. It is virtually impossible for the lone defender to keep the ball from going into the post indefinitely. This is a very demanding defensive drill and should be continued for only a short period of time. If the defensive post can intercept or deflect a pass or keep the offensive post from receiving a pass for 20 seconds, the drill is concluded and another defensive player is assigned to cover the post. Diagram 5-8 illustrates the five-on-one drill. Should the offensive post man receive the ball, he is instructed to try to score. The instant 5 catches the ball, X5 must react by moving to a position between 5 and the basket. The perimeter players are restricted to passing the ball only. When 5 shoots the ball, as in all drills, X5 is to block out and retrieve the rebound.

Diagram 5-8

Defensing the Pinning Post

Muscle, weight and strength are fast becoming important physical factors in the game of basketball. Modern coaches have discovered ways to utilize these factors when players with height have not been available. It is possible to take a big strong tackle at the conclusion of the football season and teach him something about positioning and shooting a muscle shot underneath the basket, and have him make a contribution to the basketball program.

The post offense that is built around the big, heavy, husky player usually places emphasis on the post man shaping up to receive the pass and places the responsibility of getting the ball into him on the outside players. In Diagram 5-9, 5 spreads out in his position taking up as much space as possible. He usually sets up in a direct line between the ball and the basket. The defensive post man is obligated to take one of the routes shown in the diagram. If X5 starts around 5 from the baseline side, as shown in Diagram 5-10, 5 pivots, keeping his tail against X5, and he calls for the ball in front of his nose. 2 can feed the post or can pass to 1 who will have an even better passing lane.

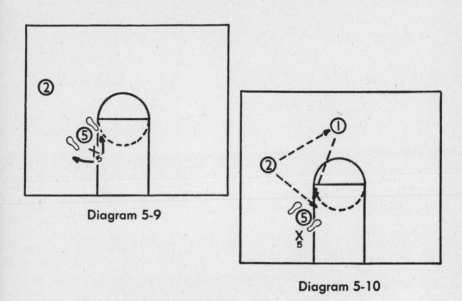

Diagram 5-9

Diagram 5-10

Should the defensive post move up to the high side of 5, 5 will pivot and pin X5, and 2 should pass the ball to the corner man, 4. If 5 holds his position, 4 will be able to feed him on the baseline for a layup as shown in Diagram 5-11.

The effectiveness of the pinning post depends on his ability to get position on the defensive man, then being able to keep that position. The outside players have the responsibility of moving the ball to the most favorable position from which to feed the post. In order for 5 to do his job as he would like to, he must make contact with the defensive post man and maintain this contact in order to remain open to receive

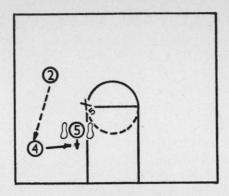

Diagram 5-11

the pass. Then, this defensive guideline naturally follows: Stay away from the offensive player—do not lean on him or make contact with him. The farther X5 can stay away from 5 and still cover him, the better.

The big, strong, post man would like nothing better than for the defensive player to get all the way in front of him. Diagram 5-12 illustrates the offensive situation when X5 moves directly in front of 5.

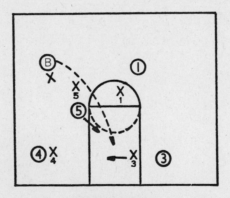

Diagram 5-12

5 will hold X5 until the ball is directly over his head, then release and go get the lob pass and have a layup. X3 should provide help for X5 on the lob. X3 must use his best judgment in providing help on the lob pass. In those cases where his anticipation and position permit, he

can aggressively play the pass. Should the passers hang the ball up in the air, X3 has as good a chance to get the pass as the intended receiver. X3 can fake as if he were going up the lane with 3 and encourage the lob, while mentally he is prepared to go after the pass. *Lob pass* is a commonly used term for the over-the-top pass, but it is actually a misnomer. The pass to the post will, in most instances, be a high straight pass and, when properly executed, gives X3 little chance of an interception. Another option in providing help is for X3 to establish his defensive position and draw the charging foul as 5 moves in to the lane to receive the pass. 5 will have his eyes on the ball, and provided X3 establishes his position early enough, the resulting contact will be the responsibility of 5. Many offensive players, upon receiving the lob, will bring the ball down to their waist and gather themselves prior to jumping and shooting the ball. This offensive error provides X3 with still another chance to help by deflecting the ball or tying 5 up for a held ball.

Defensing the Overload Set

Now, the offensive-defensive situation becomes a game of cat and mouse. The probable next move by the offense is to break 3 up to the high post as shown in Diagram 5-13. X3 is now faced with the dilemma of moving out in front of 3 and beating him to the spot at which he expects to receive the ball, or of staying back and helping on the lob. The offense is set up in an overload situation, and it presents a

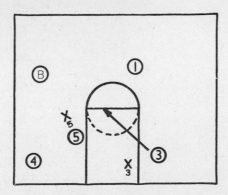

Diagram 5-13

difficult task for the defense primarily because there is no weak side defensive man to help out on the lob.

Following the basic rules, X3 should beat his man to the high post and prevent the pass into 3. The situation shown in Diagram 5-14 is a classic illustration of the importance of putting pressure on the passes. X2 should aggressively pressure 2 and prevent him from having lots of time to make his lob pass. X5 should not get locked in front of 5, but should keep moving. X3 should communicate with X1 as he moves out to cover 3 with such information as, "You are helping under the basket," or a key word such as "overload," which would indicate to X1 that he automatically becomes the single player who can help out on the lob.

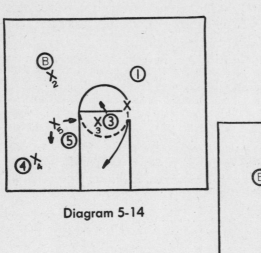

Diagram 5-14

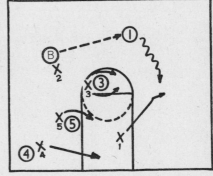

Diagram 5-15

The offense can easily move the ball to 1. This means that X1 must approach 1 and get outside of him, preventing the drive to the open side of the court. On the pass from 2 to 1 the defense should react quickly, as shown in Diagram 5-15.

The overload with all of the offensive players on one side of the court makes it impossible for the offense to reverse the ball quickly. 1 must dribble, which will give X1 more time to shape up on him, or one of the other four players must exchange sides of the court. In either event, the defensive players should have ample time to establish their proper positions after the ball is reversed.

An offensive team that has a good strong post man and that depends on the overload or the triangle formed by 2, 4, and 5, as their basic offense, would warrant special considerations in defensive post play.

Special Considerations in Post Defense

An offensive team whose primary offense revolves around post play from an overload set or the triangle formed by 2, 4 and 5 would warrant special consideration when planning the team defense. Many variations of the basic defense could be used and the decision as to which would be preferable would depend to a large extent on the strength of the other four offensive players.

In situations such as these it would be advisable to permit the ball to go into the corner. Allowing the pass from 2 to 4 would free X4 to help out on the post and would permit X5 to play beside 5, as opposed to playing in front of him. Diagram 5-16 illustrates the defensive adjustments when X4 helps on the post. X2 should drop off the ball handler in order to make the adjustment shown in Diagram 5-17 when the ball is passed into 4. X5 moves behind 5 in this instance because he has help from the outside from X2 and X4. Diagram 5-18 shows the

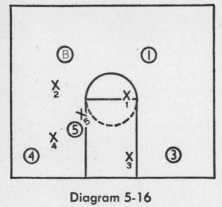

Diagram 5-16

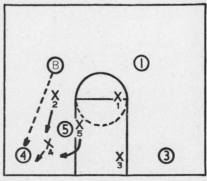

Diagram 5-17

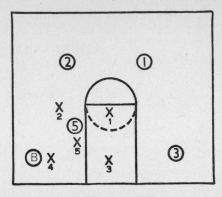

Diagram 5-18

positions of the players after 4 has received the pass from 2. Hustling scissor action by X4 and X2 can go a long way toward preventing 5 from receiving the ball. The ball in the corner affords the defense opportunities to utilize special defensive tactics. These variations of the basic defense are discussed in Chapter 10.

Diagram 5-19 illustrates a high-low post play that is effective when X3 permits 3 to receive the ball on the high post while X5 is fronting. If X3 stays under the basket to help on the lob, 3 has a free throw. If X3 comes out to cover 3 after he has received the ball, 5 can pin X5 and receive a pass from 3 underneath the basket. Permitting the pass to the corner, playing beside or behind the post, and scissoring action by X2 and X4 can eliminate this offensive threat.

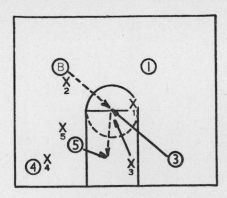

Diagram 5-19

Another possibility in defensing the triangle or overload offense is shown in Diagram 5-20. In this instance X1 drops off into the high post area and covers 3 as he breaks up. This coverage permits X3 to continue to help on the lob. The only safe pass remaining for 2 is to pass the ball to 1, as shown in Diagram 5-21. X1 must stay on the high side of 3 and not get tied up in a screen as he moves out to pick up 1. X1 must get outside 1 and prevent him from dribbling down the sideline.

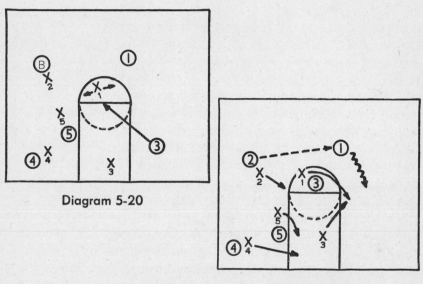

Diagram 5-20

Diagram 5-21

X3 moves up to a position between 3 and the ball, X4 hustles into the lane ready to help, X5 moves on the pass from 2 to 1 and fronts 5 as he moves toward the ball. Permitting the pass from 2 to 1 does not place the defense in too much jeopardy since 1 must wait for his teammates to move across the court in order to have a safe pass and to set up the offense again.

The best post defense is executed by a defensive player who is constantly on the move and who never makes contact with the post man. The defensive post man should be on one side of his man, then in front, back to the side, behind him, back to the side, in front, on the other side, etc. As the defensive man moves, he should be aware of the location of the ball and the proximity of the offensive player to the basket. To play post defense in this manner requires quickness, agility, determination and excellent conditioning. Playing in such a manner will frequently place the defensive man in a position to deflect or intercept the pass into the post. The ball handler becomes cautious since he cannot simply throw the ball in front of the post man's nose and expect him to go get it. This cautiousness causes the ball handler to hesitate, and the hesitation causes mistakes. The defender covering the ball handler can aid the defensive post man by applying pressure to the passer. Constant pressure on the passer, and an active defensive post man present a dismal picture to the feeder, compared to no pressure on the ball and a defensive player leaning on the post man. The image presented to the passer will produce a psychological effect conducive to bad passes and a subsequent loss of confidence.

The team defense will be planned according to the information gained from scouting reports when they are available. The absence of any prior information means that the players and coaches must make determinations as the game progresses. The information that would be most beneficial concerning the offensive post man would deal primarily with the way he contributes to the team offense. Is he basically a scorer? What are his favorite shots? Jump shot? Hook shot? Can he shoot with either hand? What position on the court does he prefer to operate in? Does he follow his shots? Does he rebound teammates' shots aggressively? Is he used primarily as a rebounder? Is he difficult to block off the boards? Does he give two and three efforts on rebounds? What does he do in the majority of instances after he receives the ball? Can he drive? Which direction does he favor? Does he fake before shooting? What are his favorite moves? Does he meet all passes? When fronted, does he pin and call for the lob? When pressured, will he move farther out on the court to receive a pass? In the team offense is he used primarily as a passer? Is he used as a screener? Does he screen aggressively? Does he roll out of his screens to the basket?

The answers to these questions will determine the best way to defense the post. Covering the scoring post by trying to keep him from receiving the ball has been discussed. Blocking out the player who is a good rebounder is discussed in the chapter on defensive rebounding. Defensing screens in various areas of the court is covered elsewhere.

If the offensive post is an adept ball handler who is used to feeding the ball to cutters, the defensive post man must be alert to pick up and help his teammates when their man gets open. Once the offensive post has received the ball, the defensive post man should loosen up and be prepared to stop the drive or to help his teammates should the ball be handed off to one of their assigned men.

The defensive post man is responsible for his man and the basket area. Any time a driver beats his man, he should be checked by the defensive post. Diagrams 5-22 and 5-23 show the defensive adjustment when the defensive center has to cover a driver. In Diagram 5-22, 1 has split the front line defense and X5 must contest him as he drives down the middle. X2 failed to close the gate and give the proper support to X1. X2 should react by moving into the passing lane and cutting off the pass to 5. X4 and X3 must react to the drive by dropping off into the lane to help where needed. The defense should crowd the basket area and force 1 to pass off to 2 or one of the corner men, 4 or 3.

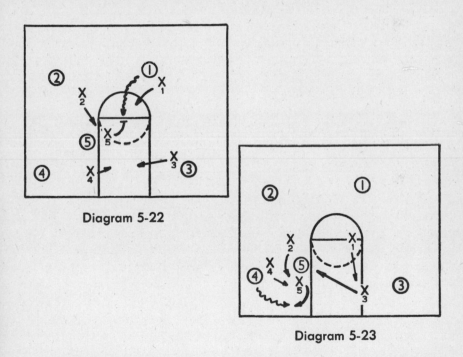

Diagram 5-22

Diagram 5-23

Diagram 5-23 illustrates the defensive adjustment when an offensive player drives the baseline. X5 picks up the driver, 4. X4 continues after 4 and double-teams with X5 after X5 has stopped the drive. X2 covers the return pass to 5 if 5 stays high. X3 checks 5 if 5 moves into the lane in front of the basket. X1 rotates and is responsible for the bounce pass underneath the basket to 3. On the shot, X3 must block out 5, and X1 must block out 3.

6

Offensive Maneuvers Requiring Special Man-for-Man Attention

Most offensive sets involve some sort of post play. One of the basic plays involving the post is the split, or two outside players cutting off the post after he has received the ball. There are many ways to split the post, and the defense must be prepared to cope with them.

In order for an offense to split the post, the ball must be passed into the post. Should this offensive maneuver comprise a major part of the total offense, the coach might want to set his defense with special emphasis on denying the pass into the post. (See Chapter 5 for a discussion of post defense.)

Diagram 6-1 illustrates the guard split off the high post. As a general rule, the player who passes the ball to the post is the first cutter—in this instance, 1. 2 then makes his cut off of 5. 5 can hand off to either cutter that is open, and the second cutter, 2, has the better chance of being open since his cut frequently is timed in such a way that he has the benefit of a double screen made by 1 and 5. If the defense decides to switch on this play, one effective technique is for X1 and X2 to drop off quickly in the lap of 5 and come shoulder to shoulder as they harass 5. As 1 and 2 make their cuts, X2 takes the player coming to his left, or 1, and X1 takes the cutter coming to his

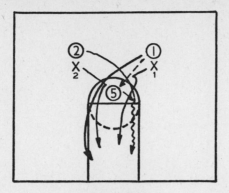

Diagram 6-1

side or to the right. As shown in Diagram 6-1, this method of defense is effective as long as both offensive players cut for the basket, and as long as they split or cross. Switching teams develop the bad habit of waiting for the offense to come to them—that is, the player guarding the screener prepares to switch men and is always expecting an offensive player to come to him off the screen. Diagram 6-2 illustrates the defensive dilemma when the second cutter, 2, cuts in the same direction as 1.

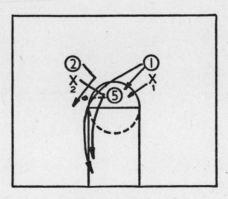

Diagram 6-2

If the defensive guards focus their attention on ganging up on 5, they leave themselves open for a return pass to their men under the basket, as shown in Diagram 6-3.

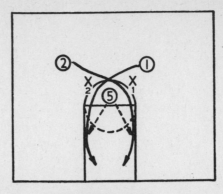

Diagram 6-3

If X1 and X2 use sliding-through techniques in defensing this play, the offensive cutters, especially the second cutter, 2, can pull up for the jump shot inside the circle, as shown in Diagram 6-4. X1 and X2 must go over the top of the screen set by 5, as shown in Diagram 6-5.

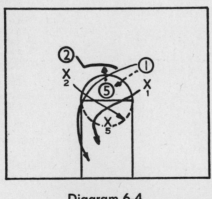

Diagram 6-4

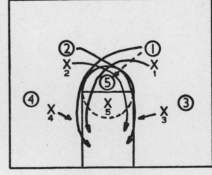

Diagram 6-5

When 5 receives the pass, X5 must retreat and be ready to help, or as a last resort switch and pick up the cutter who receives the hand-off in the danger zone designated as the basket area. As long as 5 has his back to the basket, X5 can play loose in anticipation of a drive by 5, and can be ready to help in the event X1 or X2 gets screened, and 5 hands off to 1 or 2. X5 must not be fooled by a fake pass to one of the cutters. He cannot help away from the ball, and in this situation his man, 5, has the ball. X1 and X2 fight over the screen without help from X5. X5 will help only when the ball is handed off to one of the cutters. In those instances that X5 must pick up the cutter, the man originally assigned to the cutter is responsible for the return pass to 5, if he rolls to the basket. The two defensive players assigned to players not involved in the split, X3 and X4 in Diagram 6-5, should drop off their men, toward the basket, when the ball is passed into the high post.

Diagram 6-6 illustrates the same basic split when the cutters are a guard and forward. X2 and X4 fight over the screen as previously described, and X5 loosens up after 5 has received the pass, ready to stop 5's drive or to help in the basket area should he hand off to one of the cutters.

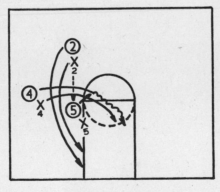

Diagram 6-6

Variations of Splitting the Post

A common method of splitting the post, used by teams that utilize their post man as a scoring threat first and a passer secondly, is illustrated in Diagram 6-7. The cutters, 2 and 4, rather than cutting close to the post, make their exchange and screen away from the post in an effort to keep their defensive men in a position such that they cannot help or gang up on the post. The basic rule for the offense is: The man who hits the post (passes him the ball) screens for his teammate. In Diagram 6-7, 2 passed to the post and has set a screen for 4. This offensive play is designed to produce a medium jump shot. In defensing this variation of the split, the basic defensive rules governing screens away from the ball are followed. X2, who is guarding the screener, loosens up and gives X4 room to slide through between him (X2) and the screen. The man loosening up, in this case X2, will find himself in position to help 5, at least temporarily.

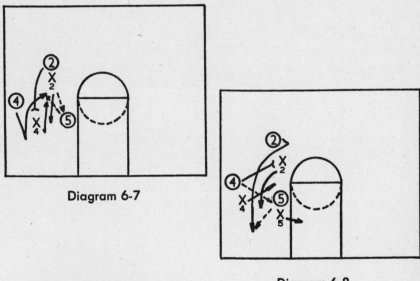

Diagram 6-7

Diagram 6-8

Diagram 6-8 illustrates this type of split when the corner man, 4, feeds the post. X4 loosens up and allows teammate, X2, to slide through the screen. X5 should be up beside 5 with the ball at 4. He should retreat quickly to a loose position between 5 and the basket when 5 receives the ball. As long as 5 has his back to the basket, the possibility of him driving presents the biggest threat to X5. If 5 pivots and faces the basket, X5 must attack and play him in the same manner that a guard would play defense on his man.

Some offenses run the split with the rule that, when the ball goes to the post, the deepest man on the ball side screens the next man up. In this case it does not matter who passes the ball into the post. Diagram 6-9 illustrates this variation of the split. 2 passes the ball to the post, but since 4 is the deepest man on the ball side, he screens for 2. X4, defensing the screener, must loosen up and let X2 slide through the screen.

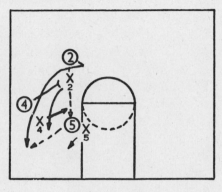

Diagram 6-9

The variation of the split that calls for both cutters to fake the scissoring or screening action, then change directions and cut in the original direction, is designed to combat the switching defense. As can be seen in Diagram 6-10, this maneuver can easily be covered with the straight man-for-man defense. The defensive players must guard

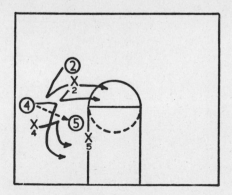

Diagram 6-10

against anticipating the screen and overplaying their assigned man. Cheating on the anticipated screens sets the defense up for the change of direction and back cut.

The High Post Rub

Almost every kid who loves the game of basketball has a goal on his garage or on a tree in the yard. Many dedicated youngsters have become proficient in two aspects of the game that can be mastered on an individual basis. The popularity as well as the effectiveness of the jump shot motivates all aspirants to work hard on this part of the game. The other phase of basketball that can be practiced on an individual basis is the art of dribbling. Endless hours of practice have produced players who are exceptional in these particular fundamentals.

The coach is quick to recognize the strong qualities his candidates possess. Consequently, it has become rather common for most coaches to include in their offensive plans special plays designed to take advantage of the special abilities of these players. The result is the inclusion of screens for the dribbler to aid him in getting open for the jump shot. Usually, these screens are set some distance away from the basket in order to keep the defense from ganging up on the shooter. This offensive maneuver will be referred to as the high post rub.

Diagram 6-11 illustrates 1 utilizing a change of direction dribble to set his defensive man, X1, up for the screen. The high post, 5, moves into a screening position and 1 rubs his man off on the screen and moves into his jump shot area for the scoring opportunity.

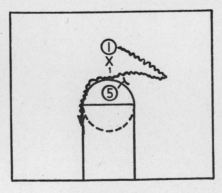

Diagram 6-11

In the event X5 switches to pick up on 1, 5 will roll out of the screen to the basket for a return pass from 1, as shown in Diagram 6-12. Should X1 slide through the screen, 1 will stop and shoot the jump shot over the screen, as shown in Diagram 6-13.

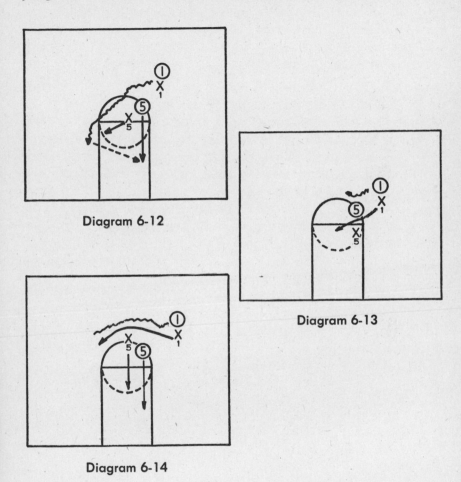

Diagram 6-12

Diagram 6-13

Diagram 6-14

The high post rub is defensed with the same basic rule as any other screen on the point of the ball that occurs inside the scoring area. Diagram 6-14 illustrates the defensive action of X5 and X1. X1 must trail the dribbler, 1, slightly as he goes over the top of the screen in order to prevent 1 from executing a change-of-direction dribble or a reverse dribble and beating him to the open side. X5 must step up and lend aggressive help to teammate X1 in order to flatten out the dribble by 1 and prevent the good angle on the attempted drive to the basket. X5 must maintain contact with 5 during this help in order to know when 5 rolls to the basket. When the contact X5 has with 5 is broken, X5 must retreat to the basket in the passing lane, with his vision focused on the basketball, in order to intercept or deflect the return pass. As 5 and X5 move to the basket, more space will be available for X1 to regain the proper position of his man, 1. X5 can help aggressively in the high post rub because his man, 5, does not have the ball.

Defensing the Blind Screen

The blind screen refers to a screen set out of the line of vision of the player being screened. Diagram 6-15 illustrates a common example of a back screen or a blind pick, as it is sometimes called. 2 has the basketball, and 4 comes up to the rear of X2 and sets his screen. 2 will drive off the screen to the open side of the court. If X4 switches and picks up 2, then 2 returns and passes to 4, rolling to the basket.

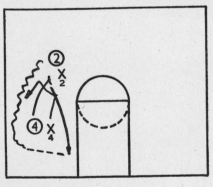

Diagram 6-15

The rules provide that when a screen is set outside the normal span of vision of the player being screened, the screener must set the screen at least one normal stride from the defensive player being screened. X2 in Diagram 6-15 should be permitted to take one step before contact occurs with 4.

Following the basic rules, X2 should be slightly to the outside of 2, forcing him to the middle of the court. X4 should warn X2 of the impending screen. This verbal communication is much more important at this point than it is when the defensive player can see the screen coming.

Diagram 6-16 illustrates the defensive action when 4 sets a back screen on X2. X2 slides even farther to the outside when he hears X4

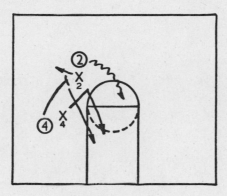

Diagram 6-16

call the screen. This movement by X2 will discourage 2 from driving to the outside. 4 will find himself in a more favorable position to set his screen to the inside of X2. 2, consequently, will be forced to use 4's screen in a way that will take him to the middle on his dribble. The drive into the middle by 2 presents a situation in which X2 can get more help from his three offside teammates. When the screen is set outside the scoring area, X2 will ordinarily slide through. However, the fact that the screen must be set about three feet from him frequently provides an easier route by going over the top. In the final analysis, results are the main objective. The defensive player is given a choice of routes outside the scoring area, provided he gets the job done.

7

How to Reduce the Effectiveness
of the Jump Shooter

The jump shot has revolutionized the game of basketball. Since its inception, the scores of games have continuously been on the increase. Youngsters emulate their idols and learn the fundamental elements of the shot at an extremely early age. Through constant practice over a period of years, many players have become proficient in the use of the jump shot, and a few have come close to perfecting the shot.

What makes the jump shot so effective? Some authorities say that the jump shot makes a big man out of a little man. In many cases this is true. There are players in the game today who can stop on a dime, go high in the air, gain complete control of their bodies at the height of their jump, and hit the basket with remarkable precision at long range. The development of strong wrists allows the shooter to hold the ball above his head on his shot. Some small players, who combine leaping ability, body control, and strong wrists, do indeed, become giants on the court.

Still another development that makes the jump shot so difficult to defense is the way in which the art of dribbling is used to get the shooter open for the shot. Dribbling, like jump shooting, is practiced almost daily by youngsters playing in their yard or driveway. The fundamentals of the change-of-pace dribble, the change of direction, and protecting the ball are developed at an early age. These basics are refined to include the behind-the-back and through-the-legs change-of-direction by all young athletes who are dedicated to the game.

The mastery of dribbling techniqes gives the ball handler more varied ways of freeing himself for the jump shot. Many years ago, the basic defensive rule was "Stay between your man and the basket." Years ago this principle presented an effective way to guard a man with the ball. If the offensive player dribbled at all, it was toward the basket. In the modern game a dribbler may be dribbling parallel to the baseline or even away from the basket and execute a quick stop and jump high in the air for an open jump shot. The dribbler can control the defensive man with a rapid dribble, forcing the defender to move at the same speed. The defensive player does not know when the dribbler will stop and go up for the shot. The defensive man simply cannot retreat with the dribbler, then react to the sudden stop quickly enough to apply sufficient pressure on the jump shooter.

Denying the Pass

There are many players who are adept at clever dribbling and good jump shooting, but many of these same players are not sound when it comes to performing the other skills involved in playing the game. One of the most glaring weaknesses common to many players is their inability to play without the basketball. A good shooter cannot make his contribution to the team unless he first receives the ball. Offensive fundamentals such as changing direction, quick stops and starts, using screens, faking, and the change of pace should be an integral part of every offensive player's repertoire. Because these fundamentals are frequently neglected, it becomes possible and often much simpler to prevent a good shooter from receiving the ball than it is to guard him after he has the ball in his possession.

Various types of man-for-man pressure can be applied to the offensive player in an effort to keep him from receiving the ball. Playing in a three-quarter position would force the offensive man to move away from the basket in order to receive the ball. It would not be out of reason to play a good jump shooter in a *tight* position at all times in an effort to keep him from receiving the ball, provided of course, that the defensive team provides the security to pick up and help when necessary. Face guarding the outstanding offensive player offers another possibility in denying him the ball. Using this technique means that the individual assigned to the outstanding shooter is relieved of all team defensive responsibilities, and focuses his complete attention on his man. The defensive man plays between his opponent and the ball and faces the offensive player at all times. The defender "dogs" the offensive player with quick reactions to his every move.

Pressuring, Forcing, and Overplaying Techniques

Many good jump shooters cannot drive to the basket. The offensive players who can drive many times are less effective with the drive than they are with the outside jump shot. A lot of offensive players have great confidence in maneuvering a defensive player in an area out on the court that gives them plenty of room in which to operate. These same players frequently try to avoid congested areas that pose the problem of being aware of more than one defensive player. Great shooters usually possess an unusual amount of concentration on the goal during their shot. This concentration frequently causes them to fail to see open teammates near the basket. These factors can influence the particular method of pressure to be applied to the jump shooter.

The first test a defender should put the offensive man through is to determine if he can drive. The defensive man can play the ball handler very closely, showing great respect for his shooting ability and very little, if any, respect for his ability to drive. Check him out—see if he can drive. If the offensive player can, and does drive, then the decision must be made as to which offensive weapon presents the biggest threat, the shot or the drive.

Scouting information should indicate the favorite shooting areas of the offensive players. If a scouting report is not available, the opponents can be studied during the pre-game warm-up in order to determine the shooting spots they favor. Once this determination is made, the defensive player should play his opponent in such a way that he forces him away from his favorite area.

Most jump shooters can hit better when they jump shoot off a dribble in the direction of their shooting hand. Right-handed shooters favor a dribble to their right when they set up their jump shot. Left-handed shooters prefer to dribble with their left hand, to their left, prior to going up for the jump shot. Players tend to emphasize the things that they can do best, and this of course would include dribbling with their dominant hand. Jump shooters practice shooting off the dribble in the direction of their dominant hand more than they do in the opposite direction. This additional practice would, at least partially, account for the greater accuracy to their dominant side. These things being true, a jump shooter can more effectively be defensed when he is forced to dribble the ball in the direction opposite his dominant hand. Forcing the jump shooter to dribble opposite his shooting hand affords the defense another advantage. It is much more awkward and takes longer for the shooter to bring the ball into shooting position and to get his shoulders squared away with the backboard when he goes up for the shot. Even more importantly, when the dribbler is moving opposite his shooting hand, he cannot provide the protection for the ball that would be possible if he were dribbling in the other direction. For example, assume a right-handed player is dribbling to his right, stops, and goes up for the jump shot. As he brings the ball from the dribble to the shooting position, the ball is naturally protected from the defensive man by the shooter's body. Now, assume a right-handed player is dribbling to his left with his left hand, stops, and goes up for the shot. In order to raise the ball to the desired shooting position, the offensive player will have to bring the ball across in front of his body. This action leaves the ball momentarily unprotected. An alert defensive man, in the proper position, will have an opportunity to play the ball as the offensive man brings it to the shooting position.

Many jump shooters have developed the bad habit of bouncing the ball before they shoot. Practicing jump shots in this manner indicates that they will hit better if permitted to bounce the ball before taking the shot. Defensively, players with this habit should not be permitted to bounce the ball prior to shooting. Offensive players who insist on bouncing the ball prior to shooting provide the defense still another opportunity to play the ball. The defensive man should quickly thrust one hand over the ball as the dribbler places both of his hands on the ball. As the offensive player moves the ball up to shooting position, he will bring the ball through the defensive man's outstretched hand.

Many times a good jump shooter lacks the speed to overpower a quick defensive player one-on-one. In these cases offensive teammates are used as screens to help free the jump shooter for his shot. When the jump shooter is hurting the defense in this manner, it is sound defensive strategy to force the dribbler away from the screen. This principle is contrary to the general rules of forcing the dribbler toward team-mates, but in isolated cases, it is more effective than depending on help from teammates.

Team Defense Against the Jump Shooter

An offensive team whose big gun is a great jump shooter poses a special problem for the defense. It is more difficult to provide help on the perimeter of the defense than it is to sag and help under the basket. When the defense is faced with an opponent who depends primarily on one player to do the majority of its shooting and scoring, the defensive plan normally does one of two things: (1) Play the regular defense and let the star get his average and hopefully reduce the output of the other players, or (2) use helping, forcing, double-teaming, and special de-fensive techniques in an effort to hold the star down below his normal output, and take a chance on the other offensive players.

There are advantages and disadvantages to each of these options. With only slight variations the team defense can be effective against an outside shooter. The best defensive player is assigned to the star. He is instructed to concentrate his efforts on the star player and not to worry too much about situations where he is to help his teammates. His teammates have the responsibility of their assigned player but *point* the star. Pointing a particular offensive man means that all of the players are aware of his ability and will be alert to situations in which they can provide help. In situations such that their responsibility is front-line support, the teammates of the defensive man assigned to the high scorer cover half of their man and half of the outstanding player. Each player in the defense is encouraged to overhelp and force the shooter to pass the ball off to a teammate, who poses less of a threat. The offensive player who shoots the ball 35 or 40 times a game will have a tendency to take bad shots and will be reluctant to pass the ball off to his teammates. A team defense that is effective in holding him to a few points will sometimes cause him to become overly concerned about his average. It is not infrequent in such instances for a selfish player to begin forcing shots and adversely affecting his team, not only on the scoreboard, but in their morale also.

Double-team opportunities within the framework of the regular defense are covered in Chapter 3. Those opportunities to double-team in the regular defense are limited to situations which present calculated risks. The philosophy of the basic defense prohibits the use of wild gambling techniques. In order to stop the outside threat posed by the greater shooter, the basic defense may have to be discarded in favor of more drastic measures. Pressure and forcing techniques can be applied to the star player. The rest of the team can provide security to the player doing the forcing by overplaying in the direction of the pointed player and taking advantage of every opportunity to help or to double-team.

Many concocted defenses have been designed for the purpose of holding down the outside scoring threat. The most common of these is the box-and-one. Four men play a box zone, and the best defensive man plays the star man-for-man. A variation of this defense frequently used is the diamond-and-one. The positions of the four zone players are changed to a diamond, and the star is played man-for-man. A variation of the one-three-one zone could be referred to as a T-and-one. The point man in the zone plays the best offensive player man-for-man, leaving the four zone players in the shape of a "T". The one-three-one zone can be used as a trapping defense, too. Rather than double-team the player with the ball, only the star player is double-teamed when he is in possession of the ball. The innovations and unorthodox approaches to special defenses are limited only by the coach's imagination.

In the final analysis the coach's decision of whether to stick with his bread and butter or to concoct a special defense can be made in terms of how much confidence he and his team have in their basic defense. A concocted defense is recommended only in those special cases in which it is evident that the opponent has overwhelmingly superior material.

Defensing Screens with the Man-for-Man

The majority of screens that take place in the course of a basketball game consist of an offensive player screening for his ball handling teammate in an effort to free him for a scoring opportunity. This chapter considers screens on the point of the ball when the screen takes place inside the area designated as the scoring area, screens on the point of the ball that occur outside the designated scoring area, and finally, screens used by offensive players in an effort to free a teammate for a pass and subsequent scoring opportunity.

Defensing Screens on the Point of the Ball Inside the Scoring Area

One of the most common and most effective methods of defensing the screen on the point of the ball is described by the terms *over the top* and *fighting through*. Over the top refers to the path taken by the defensive player guarding the man driving off the screen. The phrase means to go over the top of the screener; that is, between the defender's assigned man and the offensive player setting the screen. Fighting through, likewise, means to fight through the screen as opposed to sliding behind the screener. Fighting through further indicates that the task will not be a simple one, and that the defensive player must literally fight the screener in order to attain the desired path.

The scoring area, as previously indicated, specifies the distance from the basket in which players can shoot with a high degree of accuracy. The scoring area can be designated for particular teams in accordance with scouting reports and can be further adjusted with respect to individual players.

It is imperative that the defense use the over-the-top method of combating screens on the point of the ball inside the scoring area. There are four basic methods of defensing the screen play within the scope of man-to-man defense. The remaining options are: (1) sliding through, (2) going fourth man and (3) switching. Sliding through and going fourth man are ineffective inside the scoring area. Switching is less effective than going over the top.

Diagrams 8-1 and 8-2 illustrate the path of the defensive players using each of these methods. It can readily be seen that sliding through (Diagram 8-1) and going fourth man (Diagram 8-2) give the offensive player ample opportunity to drive off the screen and pull up for the jump shot before the defense has time to recover the distance between him and his assigned man and apply enough pressure to prevent or hinder the shot.

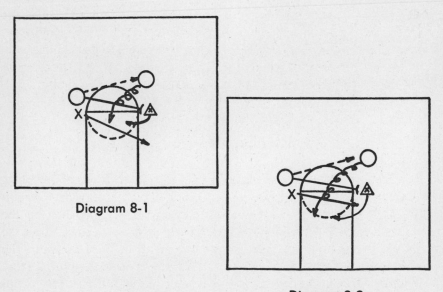

Diagram 8-1

Diagram 8-2

Switching defensive assignments offers another possibility. This method of defensing the screen play gives the defense an opportunity to apply pressure to the dribbler more quickly than the two methods previously mentioned. The pressure can best be applied by using an aggressive switch to the dribbler. This technique is commonly referred to as the jump switch. However, the shooter can still utilize the screen effectively by shooting directly over the screen. The switching method of defensing the screen leaves the defense vulnerable to several other offensive options, including the mis-match, illustrated in Diagram 8-3, and the screen and roll, shown in Diagram 8-4. The switching defense further demands greater concentration, more communication, and better execution and timing than the straight man-for-man defense. The straight man-for-man defense removes some of the need for court perception and sound judgment required by the switching man-for-man defense. Most importantly, the straight man-for-man defense eliminates the opportunities for excuses and alibis that frequently occur with the switching defenses.

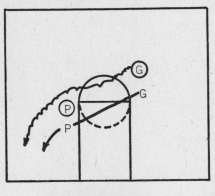

Diagram 8-3

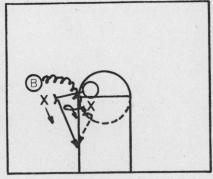

Diagram 8-4

Now to the over-the-top or fighting-through techniques involved in combating screens, hereafter to be referred to as over-the-top. Bear in mind that one of the major objectives of the defense is to apply pressure on the shooter, with the idea of reducing the number of shots taken and to apply enough pressure on the shooter to cause him to adjust his shooting style to the point that his accuracy (shooting percentage) decreases considerably. The effectiveness of the jump shooters in the game today is a cause for major concern. One of the best ways to reduce their effectiveness, once they have received the ball, is by applying all the pressure possible within the limits of sound defense.

The offensive play occurring most frequently involves a player passing to his teammate, then following his pass to screen for the receiver. Diagram 8-5 illustrates the over-the-top method of combating this basic two-man play.

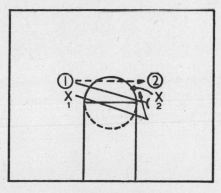

Diagram 8-5

1 passes the ball to 2 and moves to set a screen on 2's defensive man, X2. As 2 drives off his screening teammate, 1, X2 in covering 2 must take the path between the screener, 1, and his assigned man, 2. When 1 sets the screen, X1, who is guarding the screener, should communicate to his teammate who is about to be screened. X1 should call the screen with such phrases as "screen left," "screen right," or "watch the screen." X2, as he goes over the top, trails 2 slightly in order to prevent 2 from cutting back away from the screen with a dribble drive. The most important part of the technique of getting over or through the screen is the footwork of X2. In Diagram 8-6, X2

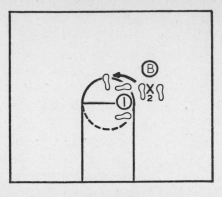

Diagram 8-6

should get his left foot in front of the screener's leading foot (also left) as his first move. Once his lead foot is positioned, X2 should raise his stance to make himself as thin as possible, and then use a quick sliding step to regain the proper position on 2. The most common and the worst mistake that X2 can make is to move his outside (right in the diagram) foot first and try to go over or through the screen with his head and shoulders leading the way. The shoulders are the widest part of the body, and therefore, the most difficult to force through the narrow space between the dribbler and the screener. Leading with the head and shoulders also places the defensive player off balance and makes him very susceptible to change of direction and reverse dribbles. Diagram 8-6 illustrates the proper footwork by X2.

X2 must slightly trail 2 over the screen. Should X2 anticipate the screen and the subsequent drive off the screen and make a premature move to get over the top, he will leave himself open for a fake drive over the screen and a cutback dribble to the open side. Diagram 8-7 illustrates the drive to the opening.

X2 can trail his man, 2, and regain position on him only when he gets the proper help from his teammate X1. When 1 sets the screen, X1 must step up to help on the dribbler, 2. As X1 assumes the helping position, he should be alert to the possibilities of tying up the dribbler, deflecting the dribble and taking the charging foul. X1 should set up as shown in Diagram 8-8, and give what is referred to as "high" help. X1 jumps quickly and aggressively into the helping position, but at the same time, maintains contact with his assigned man, 1, by touching him with his arm or hand. X1 does not hold 1, but merely feels him.

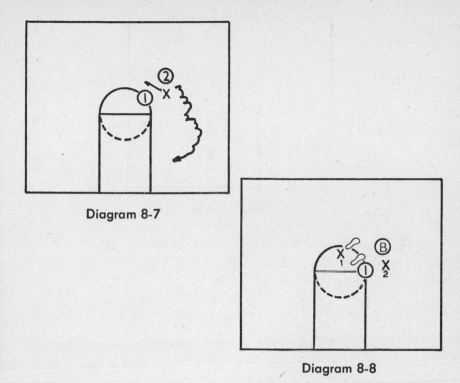

Diagram 8-7

Diagram 8-8

The high helping position will force 2 to dribble laterally across the court and will take away 2's driving angle to the basket. When 2's dribbling path is flattened out, it gives X2 more time and space in which to regain the proper position on the dribbler.

The next consideration for the defense is to prevent the return pass to 1 as he rolls to the basket. At the exact moment that 1 rolls out of the screen and begins his movement toward the basket, X1 moves with him. X1 knows to move toward the basket when he loses his contact with 1. X1 should move to the basket in a direct line between the ball and his assigned man, 1. X1's position should be open, facing the ball as he retreats toward the basket. Facing the ball increases X1's chances of intercepting or at least deflecting the pass from 2 to 1. The path of X1 is illustrated in Diagram 8-9. Moving to the basket at the proper time is very important for the proper execution of this defensive maneuver. Remember, X1 has contact with 1, and when 1 rolls to the basket, it will break this contact. The key is for X1 to move toward the basket the instant he no longer feels 1.

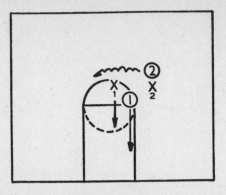

Diagram 8-9

The majority of screening on the point of the ball takes the form of the two-man play illustrated in Diagram 8-10. This is the basic screen play that must be defensed effectively.

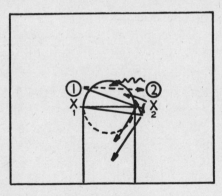

Diagram 8-10

In Diagram 8-10, 1 passes to 2 and moves to set a screen on X2. X1 moves with the screener and warns his teammate of the impending screen. X1 then jumps up aggressively into a high-help position. X2 trails his man, 2, taking away the cutback by the dribbler. X2's first step, as he fights over the top of the screen, is with his left foot, making certain that it is placed between the screen and 2. X2 then rises from his crouched stance and makes himself thin as he slides over the top of the screen. X1 maintains his high-helping position, forcing the dribbler away from the basket until he cannot feel 1. This break of

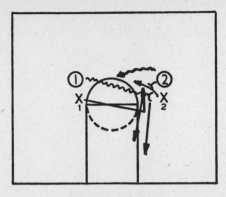

Diagram 8-11

contact indicates that 1 has rolled to the basket so X1 opens up toward the ball and retreats to the basket in a line between the ball and 1.

Most variations of the screen on the point of the ball are defensed in the same manner as described above. Diagram 8-11 illustrates a dribble screen play similar to the pass and screen play.

1 dribbles inside, hands off to 2, and screens for him. In this situation, X1 must not jump up to help until 1 has handed the ball off to his teammate. Should X1 help prematurely, 1 could keep his dribble alive and split the two defenders with a drive to the basket. Once the hand-off is made, the situation becomes identical to the pass and screen play. The same defensive techniques as previously described are applied (e.g., X1 helps and X2 goes over the top).

Diagram 8-12 illustrates a pass and go behind (outside) offensive play. Notice the similarity in this play and the pass and screen play.

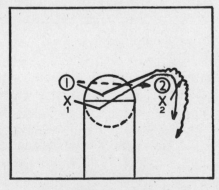

Diagram 8-12

In this instance, 2 becomes the screener and X2 must not jump help until 2 has handed the ball off to 1, coming outside the screen. 2 is alive; that is, he has a dribble coming to him and any premature movement by X2 would leave 2 an open driving lane to the basket. Also, 2 has the ball inside the scoring area and any early movement by X2 would leave 2 open for a good shot. The defense should not help off the ball. X1 must fight over the screen, trailing 1 slightly and depending on X2 to help until he can regain his normal position. Should 2 roll to the basket, X2 slides with him making certain that he is in the passing lane.

The dribble outside offensive play shown in Diagram 8-13 poses less of a defensive problem than the two previously mentioned situations since it is not necessary for the help man to time his jump with an exchange of the ball. In this case X2 can anticipate the dribbler coming over the screen and can move up to help a little sooner, provided he maintains contact with the screener and is aware of 2's move toward the basket. As in the previous situations, X1 trails his man slightly and fights over the top of the screen.

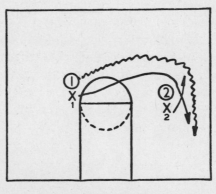

Diagram 8-13

In each of the offensive situations thus far covered, the defense is strictly man-for-man, with help given by the defensive player covering the screener. The straight man-for-man defense places the responsibility for the shot over the screen on the player originally assigned to guard the shooter. This responsibility and the additional responsibility of protecting against the cutback by the dribbler seem to be incompatible. Even with this dual responsibility, the trailing defensive player is in the favorable position to apply pressure to the shooter. An aggressive jump help from his teammate guarding the screener often occupies the attention of the potential shooter and thus discourages the shot over the screen. A very strong case can be built concerning the necessity of trailing the offensive player over the screen and stopping the cutback by the dribbler. This is an effective offensive move, and clever basketball players will be quick to recognize a defense that is vulnerable to this maneuver. In preparing to meet an opponent, it is wise to assume that they are good sound players capable of making the correct play. However, in the vast majority of cases, the player receiving the handoff continues with his dribble in the direction in which he was moving or facing upon receiving the ball. In order to present a threat in either direction, the offensive player, upon receiving the ball, must square off and face the basket. A good defensive player is quick to take notice of the habits of his opponents, and when the cutback does not pose a problem, he gets over the screen with his opponent and thereby maintains constant pressure on the ball handler.

The over-the-top defensive technique is used when combating screens on the point of the ball when the ball is in the scoring area, provided the action is taking place on the perimeter of the offense. When the offensive play involves two guards out front or a guard screening for a corner man near the sideline, the method of defense described in this chapter is used. Similar offensive plays involving post play and different cutting angles are described in other chapters. Diagram 8-14 gives some examples of perimeter play.

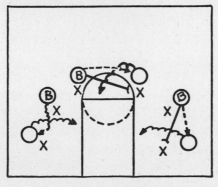

Diagram 8-14

Defensing Screens on the Point of the Ball Outside the Scoring Area

The proximity of the ball to the basket determines the defensive technique used in combating screen plays. That area which is designated as outside the scoring area is more than 20 feet from the basket and this distance decreases the percentage involved in the shooting over the screen.

The sliding through method mentioned earlier is used outside the scoring area. Diagram 8-15 helps to illustrate the details involved in this method of defense. 1 passes to 2 and sets a screen on X2. 2 drives off the screen in an effort to move the ball into the scoring area for a shot or to position the ball for a pass, etc. X2 retreats slightly and takes a path behind the screener, 1. X2 has the responsibility for guarding against the cutback, but he is far enough away from 2 that he should be able to regain his position, should 2 try to dribble to the outside. X2 slides through between the screener and his teammate, X1, and once past the screen, should move up again to apply pressure to the dribbler.

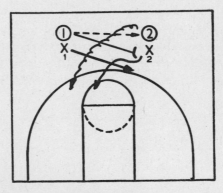

Diagram 8-15

"Slide through and move up" is the expression used to emphasize this point. X1, who is guarding the screener, calls the screen for his teammate and loosens up to allow plenty of room for X2 to slide through the screen. X1's primary responsibility is to stay out of X2's way as he slides through the screen. In the event X1 must give help, it is a sliding help as opposed to the aggressive jump help used inside the scoring area. Diagram 8-16 illustrates X1 helping. X1 helps until X2 regains his position, then X1 gets back to his man. X1 should always be

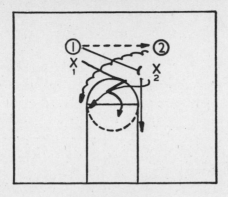

Diagram 8-16

conscious of the passing lane between the ball and his man, and should try to fill this lane as he recovers from the help position to his original man.

It will occasionally be necessary, in helping, despite all emphasis to the contrary, for X1 to move several steps with 2. It is X2's responsibility to keep working and fighting to get back to his man 2. Do not switch men in this situation. X2 must understand that it is an indication of poor defensive play on his part when X1 has to give excessive help. You must help your teammate when he needs help, and then you can expect him to help you when you get in trouble. "Help and get back" is a good coaching phrase to use throughout defensive practices. X1 must help when needed, but must exercise good judgment and avoid *overhelping*. It is a mistake to help when help is not necessary, and it is a bigger mistake to continue to help after your teammate has regained proper position on his man. Help and get back!

"Sliding through" outside the scoring area is executed in a similar manner on variations of the screen play. Diagram 8-17 illustrates sliding through when the offense uses the dribble screen. X1 loosens up and lets his teammate, X2, slide through the screen. X2 slides through between the screener, 1, and his teammate, X1, and then "moves up" to play his man 2 closely.

Diagram 8-18 illustrates sliding through against the pass-and-go-behind offensive play. In this case X2 is guarding the screener and must drop off and give his teammate, X1, room to slide through. X1 slides through between X2 and 2, then moves up to play 1 aggressively.

The dribble outside offensive option is shown in Diagram 8-19.

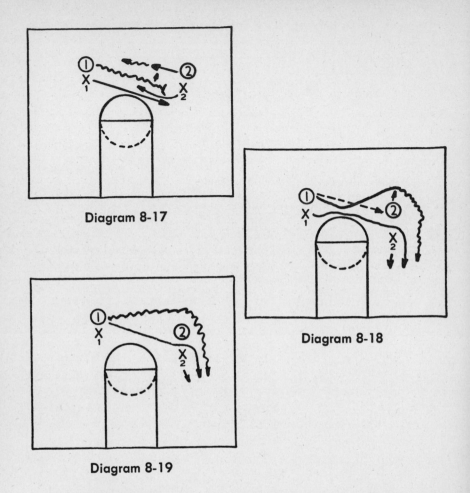

Diagram 8-17

Diagram 8-18

Diagram 8-19

Again, since 2 is the screener, the defensive player covering him must loosen up and let his teammate slide through the screen. X1 slides through between teammate X2 and the screener 2, then moves up and plays 1 aggressively.

The defensive methods and techniques described in this chapter actually make up the vast majority of the man-for-man defense. A great deal of time should be spent mastering these situations. Special emphasis is placed on knowing where you are on the court. The key to success in fighting over the screen or sliding through depends to a large extent on the communication between the defensive players and their knowledge of where they are on the court.

Defensing Screens Away from the Ball

The general rule followed on all screens away from the ball is to *slide through*. This procedure is the same as that described in defensing screens outside the scoring area. The techniques involved can best be illustrated by diagramming a few common situations with which the defense will be confronted.

The weak side exchange is an offensive maneuver designed to keep those defensive players away from the ball occupied to the extent that it distracts them from their defensive responsibilities. Diagram 8-20 shows an exchange of players 2 and 4. X2 and X4 have the responsibility of filling high and low in the lane. X2 has the primary responsibility in the high position to stop anyone attempting to drive the middle. X4 is responsible for helping the defensive post man in the event of the lob pass, and is responsible for any drives in the basket area. X2 in this situation should sag off and give ground as he

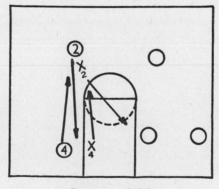

Diagram 8-20

retreats to the basket with 2. X2 has the responsibility of low weak side help and must make his first responsibility that of loosening up and making certain that his teammate, X4, has plenty of room to slide through between him and 2. X4 slides through between his teammate, X2, and the screener 2. After the weak side exchange, X2 and X4 have also exchanged positions along with the corresponding defensive responsibilities.

The high-low post exchange or high-low post screen is an offensive maneuver used by tandem post teams to free a post man for a pass near the basket. Again, since this is a screen away from the ball, the basic rule of sliding through is followed. Diagram 8-21 illustrates the defensive action taken in this situation. X5's original position is one which forms a triangle such that he can see both his man and the ball. He should be close enough to 5 to prevent the high direct pass from the wing man. As 4 moves down the lane to screen for 5, X4 must loosen up and give his teammate, X5, plenty of room in which to slide through. As 5 approaches the high post position on the lane, X5 must tighten up and assume a defensive position beside 5 on the side of the ball. X4 slides down the lane with vision in an open stance and must adjust his position depending on the location of 4. X4's new position should be one from which he can see both his man and the ball.

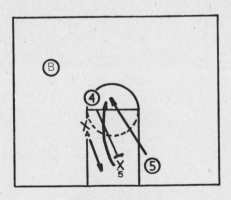

Diagram 8-21

Teams that run a three man out offense frequently pass and screen away from the pass. Diagram 8-22 illustrates this offensive maneuver and how to defense it. 1 has the ball, and the defenders, X2 and X3, are in the three-quarter defensive position. As 1 passes to 2, X3 should immediately adjust his position by dropping off his man, 3. As 1 moves in to screen for 3, X1 must loosen up and give X3 plenty of room in which to slide through. Since the screener, 1, is moving away from the ball and away from the basket, X1 should drop back in the lane, open up his stance, and be ready to help his teammates should the need arise.

If 3 comes off the screen and cuts down the lane as shown in

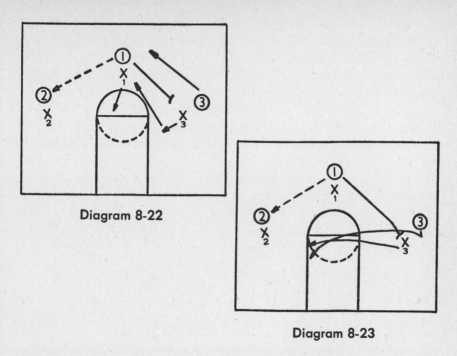

Diagram 8-22

Diagram 8-23

Diagram 8-23, X3 must slide through and then move to a fronting position on 3 as he moves toward the ball.

Defensing the Moving Screen

One of the most difficult calls for an official to make is the play involving an illegal screen. In some areas of the country officials are very reluctant to make the call at all. According to the rules, the screener must be stationary when he sets the screen. If the screener sets a legal screen, the defensive man is responsible for the subsequent contact and possible foul. When the screener moves in order to adjust the position of his screen or makes a moving screen, the screener is responsible for the contact and possible foul.

Teams that leave the middle open and do a lot of screening away from the ball frequently employ moving screens. These illegal screens are made sometimes by accident and sometimes by design. The advantage that the offense can gain as a result of moving screens places the defense at a tremendous disadvantage. Players cutting down the open middle off screens pose a major problem for the pressure-type defense.

The timing and execution of these teams must be disrupted by the defense when possible. Diagram 8-24 illustrates a simple play of the nature described that must be dealt with by the defense. 1 passes to 2 and moves in front of teammate, 3. 3 times his cut to the basket in such a way that he comes right off the tail of 1 as he moves toward the corner. X3 should loosen up when the ball is passed to 1. X1 should loosen up to allow room for X3 to slide through the screen and check 3 as he cuts for the basket. When the timing is right, X3 has a job on his

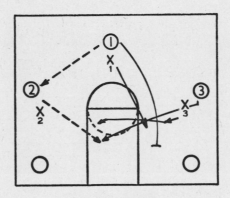

Diagram 8-24

hands. All too frequently, when X3 makes contact with the screener, he will stand straight up and stop moving in an effort to avoid the contact. This mistake can be a costly one. When the offense is moving on their screens, it is advisable for the coach or team captain to bring it to the attention of the officials. If the offense is permitted to continue the use of moving screens, the defense has but one choice. Each defensive player should be instructed to physically burst through every illegal screen. Rather than attempting to avoid contact, the defensive player should make certain that it occurs. The defensive contact with the screener must be hard, physical, aggressive contact. The contact should be so hard that the official cannot keep from seeing or hearing it. The idea is to make the official call a foul on someone. If he calls it correctly, the offense will be at fault. If he fails to call a foul, the defensive play should be so aggressive that it nullifies the attempted screen.

9

Coaching Exceptions to the Man-for-Man Rules

Within the confines of a man-for-man defense, there are many variations. Ideally, for the sake of simplicity, it would be best to follow a list of simple rules in all situations. However, the options available to the team in control of the ball are so numerous that it is impossible to effectively deal with all of them in the same manner. The offensive maneuvers discussed in this chapter represent a selection of frequently used offensive plays that present problems that can best be coped with by making exceptions to the rules.

The Weak Side Play

The two-man play on the open side of the court is one of the toughest plays in basketball to defense. The weak side play will be the term used to describe the play, and it is presented at this point because of the similarity between it and the high-post rub. Diagram 9-1 illustrates the weak side play with the point man and a pinch post.

The defensive post man, X5, must recognize the difference between this play and the high-post rub. In the case of the rub play, X5 can give aggressive help to X1, because 1 is dribbling the basketball. Diagram 9-2 shows what will happen if X5 moves up to help as 1 cuts

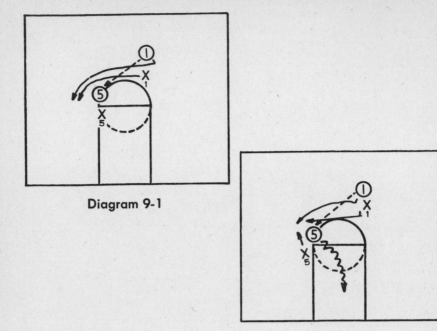

Diagram 9-1

Diagram 9-2

off the screen. 5 has the ball and is alive. Should X5 even lean toward 1 as he cuts off the screen, 5 will have the opportunity to drive to the basket. Do not help off the ball.

X1 has a much more difficult task in covering 1 as he cuts off 5 because X5 is not able to give him any help. This fact makes it necessary for X1 to fight over the screen without help, and the defensive situation facing X1 is more difficult because he cannot trail his man. X1 must get over the screen with his man.

If X1 slides through the screen, 1 will be able to take the hand-off from 5 for the jump shot over the screen, as shown in Diagram 9-3. X5's original position with the ball at 1 is the inside three-quarter position, with his right hand out to discourage the pass to 5. X5 must be careful not to overplay 5 and leave himself open for the post backdoor play shown in Diagram 9-4. X5 should make 5 work to get the ball, and once 5 has received the pass, X5 must drop off 5 far enough that he can stop any effort by 5 to drive to the basket. By leaving some space between himself and 5, X5 will be in a much better position to help X1 should the ball be handed off.

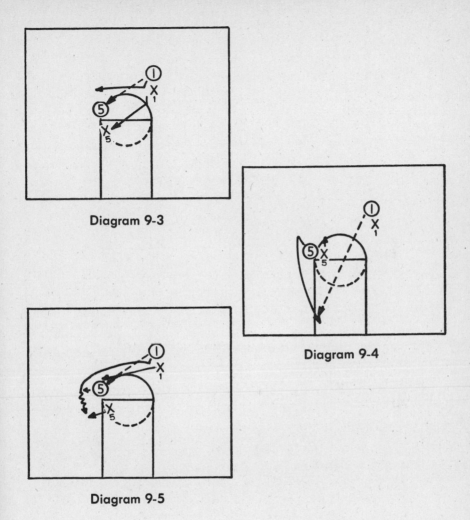

Diagram 9-3

Diagram 9-4

Diagram 9-5

Diagram 9-5 illustrates the defensive action when 5 hands off to 1. Let us review the offensive play quickly in order to have a better insight on how to defense it. 1 passes to 5 and breaks by for a possible hand-off. 5 usually pivots in such a way that he can put his hips to X1 on the screen. If 5's screen is effective, 5 will hand the ball off to 1. Of course, if X1 gets over the screen with 1, 1 would not be open, and 5 would not hand him the ball. The offense dictates the defensive techniques that will be used. When 5 hands the ball to 1, X5 will help (or switch to) 1. X5 understands that his teammate, X1, is in trouble or 5 would not have handed the ball off. The defensive post man, X5, will be with the basketball regardless of who might have possession of it. X5 cannot make a jump switch, but the instant the ball is handed to 1, he must aggressively play 1.

X1 then must continue on his path over 5's screen and work hard to get between 5 and the ball in order to stop the return pass to 5. If 5 fakes a pass and fails to hand off to 1, then X5 is responsible for the ball which is in possession of 5. X5 must stay away from 5 in position to stop the threat of a drive. The offensive post man, 5, is in the scoring area, and if he should pivot and face the basket, X5 would have to use the attack step and play him as if he were a guard.

Single Cuts off the Post

A two man play on the open side of the court, which many single post teams use, is the forward post play which operates on the same premise as the weak side play. Diagram 9-6 illustrates the offensive action involved in the forward hitting the post and cutting off the post.

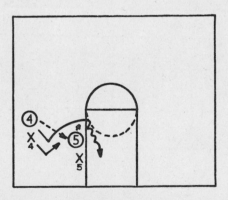

Diagram 9-6

If 4 can run his defensive man into the screen, he will be open for a good jump shot or possibly a drive for a layup. If X4 slides through the screen, 5 hands off to 4 for the jump shot over the screen.

Diagram 9-7 illustrates how many teams employ this offensive play in order to set up a walk-in for the post, 5. X5 again must stay with the ball and always remember that his man 5 is alive. No matter how much X5 is coached to "stay home" and "do not help off the ball," it

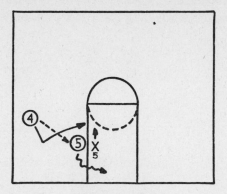

Diagram 9-7

is the most natural thing in the world for X5 to be keenly aware of 4 as he cuts off the post. If X5 as much as leans in the direction of 4, it sets 5 up for a leg cut, a bounce, and a layup or muscle shot.

This offensive move is very effective for clearing out the corner and positioning the defensive post so that 5 can use a baseline hook shot. Diagram 9-8 illustrates the defensive techniques used in defensing the forward cut off the post. X5 should make it difficult for the ball

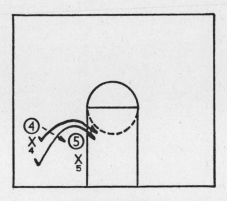

Diagram 9-8

to get into the post and should force 5 to move out away from the basket as much as possible. X4 should pressure the pass into 5. Once the ball is at the post, X4 must fight over the screen with 4. X5 will help only if the ball is handed off to 4, as this hand-off would indicate that X4 was tied up in the screen or otherwise in trouble. The defensive techniques described in covering the weak post play would apply in this case as well.

The Shuffle Cut

Bruce Drake of Oklahoma University originated the shuffle offense in the 1940's. The shuffle offense was popularized by Joel Eaves during his tenure at Auburn. The shuffle is a widely used offense today and almost every offense uses some part of the shuffle or a variation of it.

The favorite option and the most widely used is what Joel Eaves refers to as the third option of the Auburn shuffle. Diagram 9-9 illustrates the 3 man in the shuffle making the basic cut involved in the third option of the shuffle offense. Following the regualr defensive rules,

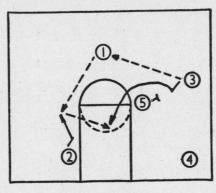

Diagram 9-9

this play should be considered as a screen away from the ball. Ordinarily, on screens away from the ball, the defense uses slide-through techniques. Team defenses vary slightly within the overall defensive plan, according to the scouting reports and other information available on the opponent. A team that uses the shuffle offense as a regular offensive pattern is defensed with the objective in mind to stop the layups and force the shuffle team to go to a secondary option.

Diagram 9-10 illustrates the action of X3 who is guarding the cutter. X3 must anticipate the shuffle cut and the screen by 5. X3

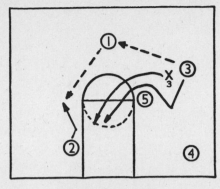

Diagram 9-10

moves over the screen on the same side of the screen that the ball is on. The pass from 1 to 2 is X3's signal to anticipate the shuffle cut and to react quickly.

The cutter, 3, usually fakes in one direction to set his man up for the screen by 5, then cuts in the opposite direction. Diagram 9-11 illustrates the cut on the baseline side of the screen by 3. The defensive man guarding the cutter always goes on the ball side of the screen regardless of which route the cutter takes. X3 moves over the screen on the key pass and continues to move into the lane area in front of the basket. X3 moves with vision ready to deflect or intercept the pass to 3. As 3 crosses the lane, X3 must shape up in the proper defensive position and continue to play him aggressively and prevent the pass into 3 in the basket area.

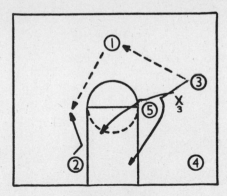

Diagram 9-11

Single post teams use a variation of the shuffle cut as shown in Diagram 9-12. Defensively, this play is considered identical to the basic shuffle cut and is defensed accordingly. X1 reacts quickly and goes on the ball side of the screen into the basket area, stopping the layup; he then shapes up on his man, 1, depending on his movement.

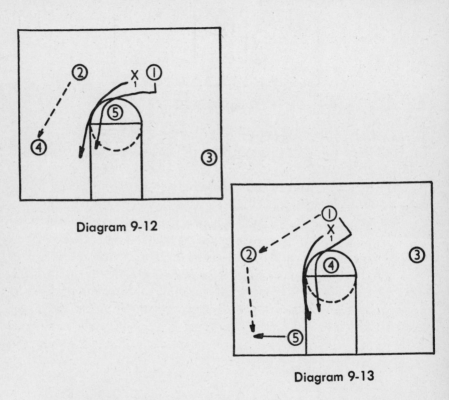

Diagram 9-12

Diagram 9-13

Tandem post teams incorporate the shuffle cut into their basic offense in the manner shown in Diagram 9-13. This offensive movement is defensed in the same way. X1 goes on the ball side of the screen set by 4, then hustles to the basket area with vision, and finally positions himself defensively according to the location of 1.

The California reverse offensive pattern, made popular by Coach Pete Newell and his great teams at the University of California, features a baseline screen. Many variations of his baseline screen have shown up in offensive systems, and the defense must be prepared to deal with this basic maneuver in a planned and organized way. In the interest of simplicity this offensive pattern is referred to as the baseline shuffle cut and dealt with appropriately. Diagram 9-14 illustrates the baseline shuffle cut and the defensive action involved. X4 goes over the high side of the screen set by 5, regardless of the path of 4. X4, anticipating the baseline screen, moves quickly over the screen, beating 4 into the lane on the ball side. X4 continues to front 4 as long as he is in the basket area.

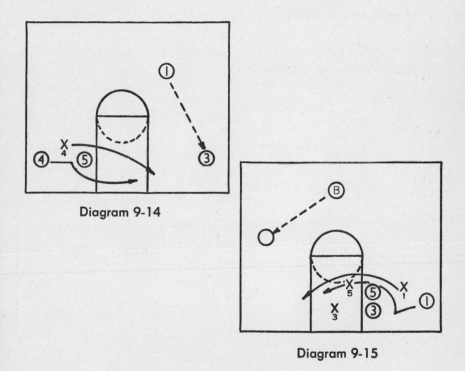

Diagram 9-14

Diagram 9-15

In describing the defensive methods of covering the particular offensive plays considered shuffle cuts, emphasis is placed on the action of the defensive player responsible for the cutter. It is assumed that the other four defensive players are following the basic rules of positioning, helping, etc.

The double screen on the baseline presents a situation similar to the baseline screen, and in general terms, is defensed in the same way. In Diagram 9-15, 5 and 3 set a double screen for 1 who cuts over the top of the double screen. X1 anticipates the cut, beating 1 over the screen and stopping the pass for the layup; he then assumes the proper defensive position depending on the subsequent action of 1. X5 and X3 are in favorable positions to provide help for 1 on this play. X5 must protect against the direct pass to 5, but X3 can move across the lane to help X1. X3 can move across the lane to help X1 as long as he or X5 is in a position to defend against the direct pass to 3 underneath the basket.

Normally, when X1 takes the high route on the ball side of the double screen, 1 will cut to the baseline side of the screen. Because of the longer distance involved for X1 going over the top of the screen, X3 must help X1 until he can gain the proper position on his man. Diagram 9-16 illustrates 1 cutting baseline, and X3 helping until X1 has time to shape up defensively.

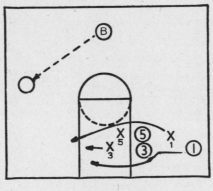

Diagram 9-16

Defensing the Weave

Teams that depend on three or more offensive players to weave the ball in an effort to set up a scoring opportunity pose a special problem for the defense. Normally, the team that weaves the ball tries to get a scoring opportunity as the result of a drive off the weave. When the drive down the middle does not open up, the offense continues the weave continuity in an effort to push the defense back inside the head of the circle, thus presenting an opportunity for a medium jump shot.

The most effective method of stopping the weave continuity is the jump switch. The switch of defensive assignments violates the principles of the basic man-for-man defense. The switch is used only against teams whose basic offense revolves around the weave. In order to simplify the defensive techniques and at the same time further confuse the offense, only designated defensive men are allowed to make the switch. Usually, the two men who play the guard positions are similar in size and quickness. These two players have an added advantage in having many occasions to cooperate both offensively and defensively. Making a switch in defensive assignments will only present another situation where these two players must use their court savvy to improve the overall team play.

There are several kinds of defensive switches that could be used. The method most effective against the weave is the box switch or jump switch. The jump switch is a premeditated defensive move in which the defensive man guarding the dribbler leaves the dribbler and jumps up in the path of the offensive player receiving the hand-off. Diagram 9-17 illustrates a jump switch between X1 and X2 that takes place outside the scoring area. X1 jumps up into the path of 2 as he receives the hand-off from 1. X2 switches to 1, and since this switch takes place outside the scoring area, X2 assumes a position between 1 and the basket.

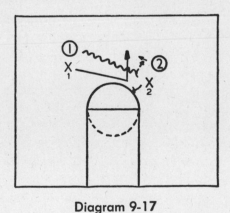

Diagram 9-17

Diagram 9-18 illustrates the same play taking place inside the scoring area. X1 jumps up into the path of 2 as he receives the hand-off, and X2 gets a position between his man, 1, and the ball. Since the play occurred inside the scoring area, X2 must take the route over the top even though there is a switch. One of the offensive plays which is

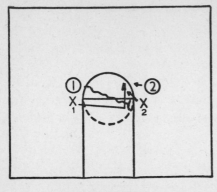

Diagram 9-18

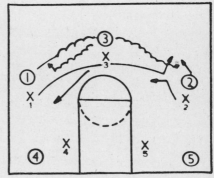

Diagram 9-19

difficult to defense occurs when 2 shoots directly over the screen. The switch does not actually occur until 2 bounces the ball. If 1 rolls to the basket, X2 must back up with him, watching the ball as he retreats. Most good offensive players will receive the hand-off from 1, stop, and pivot facing the basket, thus posing a threat to jump shoot or drive in either direction. The defense is making a calcualted risk that 2, upon receiving the ball, will continue in the same direction. When 2 continues in the same direction and tries to use the screen set by 1, X1, by utilizing the jump switch, should be able to do one of these things: (1) play the ball and tie up 2, (2) play the ball and deflect the dribble, or (3) establish position quickly and draw the charging foul.

Only the guards or other players designated by the coach will use the jump switch. This rule has the dual effect of simplifying things for the defense and complicating them for the opposition. The basic man-for-man rules are followed by all defensive players except when the designated players are both involved on the ball in the weave continuity. In Diagram 9-19, X1 and X2 are the guards who are designated to execute the jump switch against the weave continuity. 3 dribbles toward 1 and hands off to 1. X3 loosens up, permitting X1 to slide through. 1 dribbles toward 2, who comes to meet the ball on the weave. Now, X1 and X2 are involved in the screen on the ball, and X1 executes the jump switch to 2 while X2 gets position between 1 and the basket.

10

Coaching Variations of the Man-for-Man Defense

The basic man-for-man defense can be varied in many ways. It is preferable to run the basic defense with slight variations rather than risk overloading the team with the requirement of learning several completely different defenses. Diagram 3-2 illustrated the numbering system for varying the point at which the defense will pick up their men and apply pressure. Changing the assignment of the man covering the offensive player making the throw-in can further vary the defense. The score and time remaining in the game will dictate the use of more drastic measures on occasions. The defense must be prepared for all possible situations which may confront them in the course of a season. This chapter is concerned with the variations of the basic defense and when to use them.

The Full-Court Man-for-Man Press

It is advantageous to press opponents who individually do not possess the ability of the defensive team. Teams which know they are outmanned resort to all types of wild tactics in an effort to make a good showing. Against weak opponents, one should expect and be prepared to play against a ball control offense and some sort of unorthodox zone or stunting defense. The more of the court area these opponents can be forced to play on, the greater the opportunity to take advantage of your individual superiority.

The full-court press is designed to force the opponents to play offense from baseline to baseline. The same principles used in the basic defense apply, only now over the entire court. Diagram 10-1 illustrates the positions of the players using a 95 defense. X2 will permit 2 to receive the inbounds pass provided he moves to catch the ball. X2's defensive position is like the position described in defensing the strong side forward. X2 should play the three-quarter position and make certain that 2 does not move down the court and receive a long pass over X2's head. Once 2 has received the inbounds pass, X2 has the responsibility of guarding the dribbler, as described in Chapter 2. He must not let the dribbler beat him—no matter how much ground he gives up. X2 will force the dribbler to change directions as many times as possible as he dribbles the ball up the court. X2 will favor the sideline and keep 2 out of the middle as he dribbles up the court. X2 applies all the pressure he is capable of putting on 2, but must never overpress and permit the dribbler to get by him. X2 plays the man, not the ball—the dribbler, not the dribble.

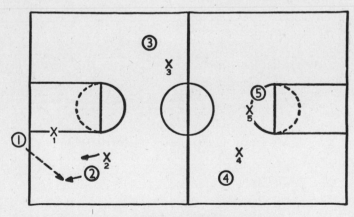

Diagram 10-1

Most offensive teams, when confronted with a full-court man-for-man pressing defense, get the ball inbounds to their best ball handler and have the other four players clear out. Many times the best dribbler on the offensive team is also the best, or one of the best, scorers on the team. The defense, by applying constant pressure on this offensive player throughout the game, can cause him to become fatigued and greatly reduce his effectiveness toward the end of the game. The defense can use two or more defensive players to alternate on the assignment of covering the dribbler.

Diagram 10-2 shows 2 dribbling the ball up the right sideline and the subsequent positions of the other four defensive players. Notice that X1 is on the line of the ball ready to help if 2 moves into the middle with his dribble. All defensive players should be as deep as the ball. The defense will concede any pass away from the basket they are defending, such as a pass from 2 back to 1. X4 is pressuring the sideline pass to 4. His defensive position is slightly different than that explained for defensing the strong side forward because he is adjusting his position in accordance with the basic rule: The farther your man is from the ball, the farther you can play from him. The position of X4 is one from which he can get to the ball in the event the sideline pass is made. X4 is closer to the ball than the three-quarter position would permit and consequently is in a better position to cover 4 if he moves up to meet the pass. The defensive position of X5 is a fronting position from which he can see both 5 and the ball. He too, because of the distance of 5 from the ball, can move closer to the ball. 3 is the farthest offensive man from the ball, and this allows X3 to drop off toward the basket and be ready to help. X3 should not be so far from 3 that he cannot intercept the pass from 2.

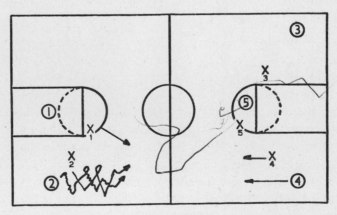

Diagram 10-2

Diagram 10-3 illustrates the defensive adjustments that would be made if 2 picked up his dribble. When 2 picks up his dribble, the "tight" situation is on. X2 attacks 2 and pressures his pass. X1 closes out on 1 into the passing lane since he is relieved of helping responsibilities. X3, X4 and X5 move into the passing lane on their man. Each of them can take more chances now as they will not be required to help on the dribbler. Pressure defense is a five-man proposition, and the tight situation will test the fortitude of each of the players. The defense has an excellent chance to intercept or deflect the next pass. If X1, X3, X4, and X5 maintain their positions between their man and the ball, the only way the offense can hurt the defense is on a backdoor play. If X2 applies aggressive pressure, this pass will be a difficult if not impossible one.

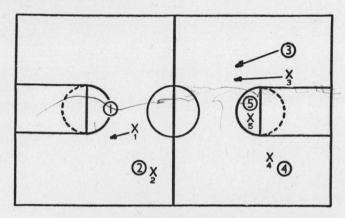

Diagram 10-3

The situation described is the most favorable one the defense could have. It is preferred to the trap set by two men in the zone presses simply because with one man covering the ball handler, all four of the potential receivers can be covered. The offense will not often accommodate the defense by picking up their dribble in the back court. The defense is trying to force this situation, but a good ball handler will be able to move the ball across the ten-second line into the front court. Eventually, the defense will force the dribbler to pick up his dribble, or the dribbler will decide to pick up his dribble. In either event the resulting tight situation gives the defense an opportunity for an interception.

Variations of the Full-Court Press

The 95 defense can be varied by adjusting the position of X1 on the throw-in. X1 can play 1 normally (Diagram 10-4), or he can pressure him on the throw-in (Diagram 10-5). X1 could double-team with X2 in an effort to make 3 or some other offensive player handle the ball (Diagram 10-6). X1 could drop off into the area of the foul line and double-team after the throw-in (Diagram 10-7). In each of these variations, X1 must release and pick up 1 when 1 advances to the line of the ball. These variations involve only the position and play of one man, but can easily pose a problem for the attacking team. The offense cannot be certain about the particular kind of press it is attacking when X1 adjusts his position.

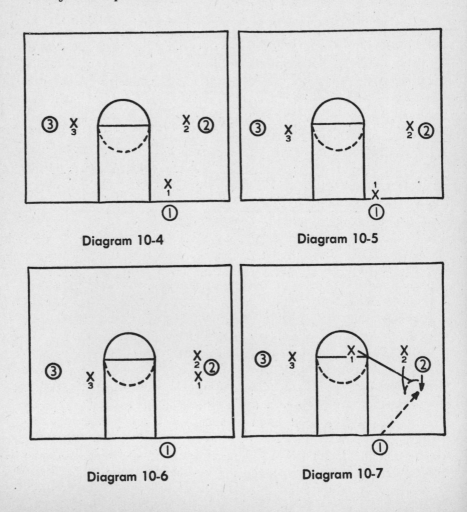

Diagram 10-4

Diagram 10-5

Diagram 10-6

Diagram 10-7

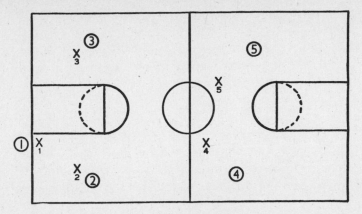

Diagram 10-8

The press out or blitz defense is numbered 100. This variation of the full-court press can be effective if it is used sparingly. The blitz is most effective as a surprise defense. The best time to use the blitz is immediately after the opponents have committed an offensive mistake that cost them a layup. The recovery of a fumble, or the interception of a bad pass by the defense, will place the opposition at a psychological disadvantage, which frequently sets the stage for a second error. The 100 defense amounts to playing tight on the throw-in. Each player executes his responsibility as he would in a tight situation. Diagram 10-8 illustrates X1 pressuring 1 on the throw-in, and each of the other four defensive players in position to intercept the pass to their assigned man. The blitz, in addition to being an effective surprise defense, becomes mandatory in the late stages of a game when the defensive team is on the short end of the score. The 100 defense, like the 95, can be varied by having X1 change his original position and assignment.

The Sagging Defense

There could be times in the course of a game when it would be strategically advantageous for the defense to drop back under the basket in an exaggerated sag. Such a situation could exist when the opponents are notoriously poor outside shooters. Perhaps, with a comfortable lead in the second half of a game, it would be wise to sag off under the basket and give the opponents the one outside shot. Such defensive tactics might also keep a player in foul trouble from committing additional fouls.

In situations where it is desirable to sag, the defensive adjustments that need to be made involve two basic rules: (1) the point at which pressure will be applied, and (2) pressuring only the shooter in the designated area and permitting the ball handler to make his passes unmolested. Diagram 10-9 illustrates the positions of the players in the sag or "O" defense. X2 does not apply pressure on the ball handler, 2. X4 concedes the pass to the corner. X1 and X3 drop off their men and fill the middle. X5 is beside the post man but moves behind him as he adjusts his position on the movement of the ball or when 5 moves.

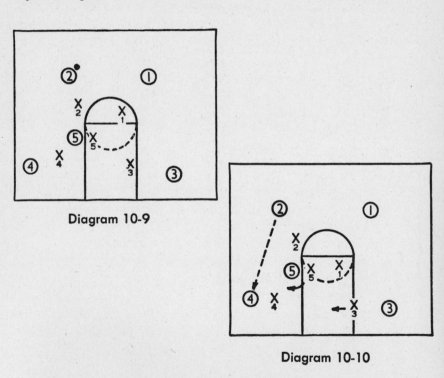

Diagram 10-9

Diagram 10-10

Diagram 10-10 illustrates the defensive adjustment when 2 passes the ball to 4. This exaggerated sag is played with the idea of not only permitting but encouraging the outside shot or the shot out of the corner. The defensive post man will be behind 5 in most instances. X5's primary responsibility is to block 5 off the board when the outside shot is taken. X1, X2, X3, and X4 must help X5 from the outside in

—that is, they drop off their man and concentrate their efforts on pre-venting the ball from going inside. The offense must not be allowed to pass the ball inside. They must not be permitted to drive to the basket, and above all, they must be limited to only one shot. The final and most important responsibility of each defensive player is to block his assigned man off the boards and make certain he does not get an offensive rebound.

Keeping the Offense from Reversing the Ball

In order for an offense to maintain continunity, the ball must be taken from one side of the court to the other. An offensive team that depends on patience and continuity to produce the desired scoring opportunity can be forced into secondary options by preventing the ball from being passed around the horn.

The shuffle offense is a common example of an offense that is built around ball control and a continuity pattern. One version of the shuffle offense is shown in Diagrams 10-11 and 10-12. Continuation of

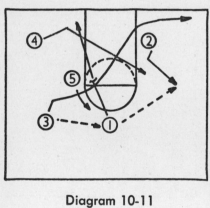

Diagram 10-11

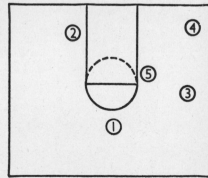

Diagram 10-12

the movement of the ball and the players in this pattern would eventually have all five offensive players play each of the positions shown. It can readily be seen that the players progress from spot to spot in the following order: 1 moves to 2 position, 2 becomes the 3 man, 3 moves into the corner and fills the 4 spot on the opposite side of the court, 4 moves into the post area and becomes the post or the 5 man on the opposite side, and 5 moves off the screen by 1, into 1's position. The basketball must be passed from the 3 man, to 1, to 2 in order for the offensive pattern to function properly.

Diagram 10-13 illustrates the two passing lanes that must be open for the offense to reverse the ball. The pass from 3 to 1, or from 1 to 2, must be stopped or at least delayed. Should the first pass from 3 to 1 be completed, then the passing lane from 1 to 2 can be blocked. If the defense applies sufficient pressure, hopefully, one of the following things will happen: (1) The pass will be intercepted, (2) the pass will be deflected, (3) the pass will be delayed, (4) the receiver will be forced into a new position in order to receive the pass, or (5) the pass will be prevented.

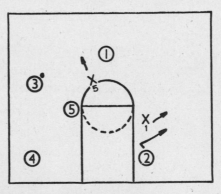

Diagram 10-13

Should the offense run a pattern that moves the ball from corner to corner, one or two additional passes must be made, thus giving the defense additional options to playing the pass. Diagram 10-14 illustrates the different points at which the defense can close off the passing lanes in order to prevent the ball from moving from one side to the other. The particular pass the defense attempts to cut off would depend on the offensive characteristics of the opponents. Normally, the pass

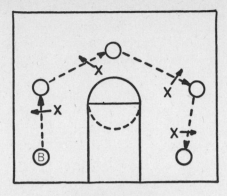

Diagram 10-14

out of the corner, or the pass to the middle, presents better opportunities to the defense.

The defense does not have to intercept the pass for their tactic to
be successful. If the pass is prevented, the offense is obligated to resort
to secondary options. Making the offense do something that it would
prefer not to do is good defense. If the pass the offense wants to make
is delayed because of the defensive pressure, the timing involved in the
continuity offense is disrupted, and the defense has been effective. If
the potential pass receiver is forced to move away from the basket or
into an undesired area in order to receive the pass, the defense has
forced him to make his move from a position other than the preferred
one. Keeping the offense from reversing the ball provides additional
time for defensive adjustments.

Team Defense Based on Opponent's Personnel

The basic team defense involves a definite five-man plan depen-
dent on the coordination of the individual effort of the players. Each
player is aware of what the others are doing at all times. The same
basic rules apply to each and every defensive player regardless of his
position or assignment. The team concept provides defensive security
and the confidence that comes with knowing you can depend on the
cooperation and help of your teammate. The basic man-for-man defense is designed to defend against a good offensive unit composed of
five complete players who are fundamentally sound in all phases of the

game. The basic defense is an overall plan that would be effective on any night against any opponent. The defense is planned in such a way that it can be used to pressure opponents who want to hold onto the ball, and still not extend itself to the point that it becomes a gambling type of defense.

The basic man-for-man defense has the built-in advantage of being able to match up the defensive players against appropriate offensive players. It does not, however, take into full account the individual strengths and weaknesses of the opposition. Further, it does not consider the team tendencies or habits of the individual offensive players. The information gained through films, scouting reports and other sources could very well dictate several appreciable changes in the basic defensive plan.

The most important information contained in a scouting report relates to the individuals on the opposing team. The defensive man assigned to a specific opponent can do a much better job when he has an idea of what to expect. The regular defense can be improved by taking advantage of the information available on the opponent. The most effective variation of the basic defense is one which is designed to defense each individual according to his strengths and weaknesses.

The adjustments in individual assignments must be understood by the entire team. When the defense makes adjustments to compensate for the individual strengths and weaknesses of the offensive players it will be difficult in many cases, and impossible in some, to remain with the concepts of the basic team defense. The recommended method of teaching this defensive variation is to have the freshman team or taxi squad play the part of the opposition. Players selected to represent opponents should be selected on a basis of the similarity in size and playing habits to the individuals that make up the opponent's team. The best way to illustrate the variation of the basic defense in accordance to the personnel of the opponent's would be to offer an example of the highlights of a scouting report and the subsequent match-ups and variations of each defensive player. The following report is abbreviated and omits information other than that which would apply in setting the defense.

Podunk U. Personnel

#30 ROBERT BORDER—6'7" Junior—160 pounds—one year letterman—scoring average, 20 points—excellent shooter from 16 feet out—when he has the ball out of his range, will penetrate through middle to within his range and shoot—jumps forward on his jump shot—can make him commit charging foul—excellent offensive rebounder, works for position on offensive board —MUST BE BLOCKED OFF BOARD—hungry and he likes to score, seldom kicks off after receiving ball—has good speed —will go for long pass, quick moves, and quick shot—will drive left with right hand—has special offensive move to middle to get open for jump shot—he is easily irritated—has a bad attitude—he is selfish—he gets upset when he is not scoring.

#44 PHIL HARRISON—6'7" Center, Guard, Forward—220 pounds—very strong and very good on offensive and defensive rebound—leads the conference in rebounds with 20.6 rebounds per game—good jump shooter from 17 foot range. Goes to offensive board from guard position HARD—likes to hook left and right—makes all throw-ins from out of bounds—very good vision—will make the long pass—will dribble ball down against press—usually lines up as guard—plays every position in offense—fair speed—likes to take one bounce prior to jump shot—VERY GOOD REBOUNDER AND MUST BE BLOCKED OFF BOARD.

#10 RICHARD DOTSEN—6'3" Junior—Guard—very good speed—will snowbird often—gets out on break quickly—good shooter from 20 feet, but will look for the drive first (usually a baseline drive)—will drive recklessly—vulnerable to offensive foul on layups, etc.—likes to take guard to post—will rebound and start fast break with dribble—will take ball all the way on the dribble.

#22 SKIP CARLSON—6'4" Senior—Guard—180 pounds —excellent outside shooter from 22 feet—looks for the jump shot—hungry—gunner—snowbird—good speed—not a threat to drive—does not rebound aggressively.

#34 TOM WILLIAMS—6'5" Senior—Forward, Post—220 pounds—strong—quick—excellent rebounder—MUST BE BLOCKED OFF BOARD—offensive talent outside questionable—poor outside shooter, gets points off board and break—good team man—unselfish—great attitude—plays to win from both ends of the floor—will drive left with right hand.

#14 MICHAEL WHEELER—6'0" Freshman—Guard—same type of player as DOTSEN, but a better outside shooter—has good moves to the basket—first sub outside.

#12 ARCHIE BROWN—6'5" Sophomore—Post, Forward—first sub inside—165 pounds—good speed—likes to line up on post —better post player than outside—aggressive—good rebounder—gets most of his points on rebounds and close shots.

Podunk University
General Offensive Information

Podunk depends on the fast break and the long pass for most of their scoring opportunities. They gamble on defense and break off from interceptions and recovery of loose balls. They cheat on the fast break from a rebound—frequently send a player to the offensive end on the shot. They like to throw the long pass to the snowbird. Podunk has good size and leaping ability and depends on the second and third shots for many of its points. They send four and five men to the offensive boards. If they do not get a fast break, they will shoot the ball after one, two, or three passes.

Podunk's Offensive Pattern

Podunk sets up in a single post offense. They rotate the players in such a way that any player might be playing in any position. When the ball is reversed to the weak side, they use a split away from the ball and move into position to keep the continuity (Diagram 10-15).

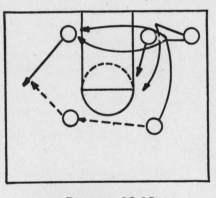

Diagram 10-15

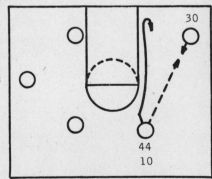

Diagram 10-16

Harrison, 44, will post when he passes to the weak side corner. Dotsen, 10, likes to use this move to take his man to the post (Diagram 10-16).

When Border receives the ball in the corner, he likes to make his move to the middle and penetrate into his jump shot range (Diagram 10-17).

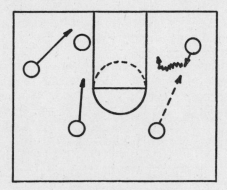

Diagram 10-17

Harrison uses this move to get rebound position from the guard spot (Diagram 10-18).

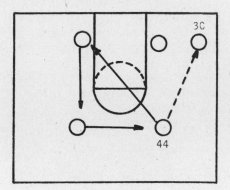

Diagram 10-18

After a basket or on a rebound, Border, Williams and Carlson will race for the lanes wide—THEY ARE LOOKING FOR THE LONG PASS AND THE QUICK SHOT—the winners of the race will screen for one another—the screener becomes the strong post and the other becomes the corner man—Harrison makes all throw-ins to Dotsen or another guard—the ball is passed back to Harrison, and he dribbles the ball up to a strong side guard position—he will make the pass to the corner or post from any position on the floor (Diagram 10-19).

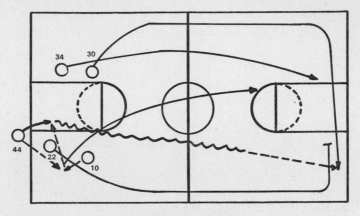

Diagram 10-19

Defensive Plan for Podunk U.

1. We must get back on defense quickly and stop their fast break.
2. Our safety should cover the snowbird and prevent them from getting an easy basket from the long pass.
3. We must block out and prevent the second and third shots.
4. We can fast break Podunk after a rebound, because they send four and five men to the offensive boards.
5. When we stop Podunk's fast break, they lack patience and will shoot the ball after a couple of passes. This means we will not have to play defense for a long period of time when they gain possession, so, get position—be alert for the long pass—work hard on defense.

Defensive Assignments

Kreier—You have #30, Border—he usually sets up in the right corner. Make him work to get the ball—if he receives the ball on the sideline or deep in the corner, be ready for his move to the middle—Border will dribble to his right with his left hand—play the ball if he fails to protect it. When he goes up for his jump shot—hang in there in position—and let him jump into you and foul. You must hustle back on defense as he will leave before his teammates have the rebound. He is all offense—he is a good offensive rebounder because he likes to score—he is quick, agile and a good leaper—he must be blocked off the offensive boards.

Lister—Your man is #44, Harrison—we expect them to play

Harrison at a guard position most of the time in order to pull you away from the basket. Drop off and be ready to help and to rebound when Harrison does not have the ball. When he has the ball inside 17 feet, you have to get on him. Do not worry about it if he gets a couple of buckets from outside—he will not beat us from out there. Block him off the boards or beat him to the ball on rebounds.

White—Your man is #34, Williams—he will be close to the basket most of the time, so this will keep you in pretty good rebounding position. The strongest part of his game is rebounding—block him off the boards! When he moves outside, let him go—look for a chance to help on Border, Harrison or Dotsen. When Williams gets the ball, he will drive left with his right hand—be alert to play the ball if he fails to protect it. Your job is to rebound and help your teammates.

Moss—You have #10, Dotsen—he is big and strong—has good speed. He is a good driver—goes hard for the bucket—favors the baseline—get one foot on the line and he will run over you. He can hit from 17 feet in, but looks for the drive first—he beats the defense with his quickness—not clever dribbling—he will take his man to the post—front him if he takes you inside—he is a good jumper and rebounder—when he gets a defensive rebound, he dribbles the ball quickly up the middle of the court. When he sees his teammates get a rebound, he takes off for the long pass.

Cockrel—You have Skip Carlson. He will hurt us in two ways —outside shooting and on the fast break. Play him tough—when he is one pass away from the ball make him work to get the ball—play him very aggressively when he does get the ball —forget about him driving and pressure his outside shot. Drop off and be ready to help when Skip is away from the ball. Do not worry about blocking out—get inside and double on Harrison and Williams. Do not let him beat you up the court for an easy shot.

Moss—Cockrel—Mike Wheeler is the first sub at guard and will replace Dotsen and/or Carlson. Mike has more maneuverability with his drive and can shoot from outside. He will not take you under like Dotsen—cannot shoot as well from outside as Carlson—but you must respect his drive.

White—Lister—Kreier—Archie Brown is the first sub on the front line. He is very aggressive—a real hustler and an excellent rebounder. He gets his points off the board—block him out. He will not shoot unless he is wide open. Play him the same way you would Williams.

Davis—You could end up covering Dotsen or Carlson.

Battle—You will be matched up with Border when you go into the game.

The information contained in the scouting report is mimeographed and handed to each player on the team. The taxi squad or freshman team is assigned to play the part of Podunk U. Each taxi squad member wears a jersey to correspond to the player he represents. The taxi squad is taught the Podunk offense. The defensive match-ups and assignments are made. Now, the defense is ready for a controlled scrimmage. Podunk is awarded the ball, and each player covers his assigned man in accordance with the information previously provided to him. The coach stops the scrimmage to point out mistakes and to help the defensive players recognize opportunities to help, etc. He constantly reminds them of the team objectives for stopping Podunk. Once the defense is familiar with Podunk's offense and with what to expect from each of their players, the Podunk team is placed on defense. Against this particular opponent the greatest amount of practice time should be spent on the defensive break. When Podunk recovers the rebound and starts their fast break, special emphasis is placed on the defensive break, getting back with vision, being ready to intercept the long pass, stopping the dribbler, etc.

The discussion of Podunk U. should provide an example of varying the team defense in accordance with the opponent's personnel.

Stunting Variations When the Ball Is in the Corner

The man-for-man defense is a basically sound defense built on time tested principles that have proven to be effective. Stunting defenses, on the other hand, are unorthodox techniques that are used primarily as a surprise tactic, or they are designed for a specific opponent. Stunting defenses are sometimes used as a special strategy against an opponent that is so superior that standard procedures would not be effective. Simply because the stunting defense is unusual, it sometimes catches an opponent unprepared and serves as an equalizer. The stunting defense is effective primarily against teams that are not fundamentally sound in individual offensive play. Coaches whose teams violate the basic principles of team offense are also susceptible to stunting tactics.

There is argument for and against such tactics. One of the glaring weaknesses of stunting is that when such tactics are unsuccessful, the defense is employed in such a way that it is difficult, if not impossible, to protect the basket. There are situations on the court that would present an opportunity to use stunting tactics and still protect the basket. Such a situation exists many times when the offense passes or dribbles the ball to the corner on the baseline. The position of the ball on the court limits the directions in which it can be passed or dribbled. With the ball in the corner offensive players on the opposite side of the court have isolated themselves and do not present an offensive threat.

Diagram 10-20 illustrates the alignment of the basic man-for-man defense when the ball is in the corner. 1 and 3 in the diagram do not pose a threat—in fact, the defense has done well if it can force a diagonal pass from 4 out to 1. X2 has the responsibility to help if 4 drives to the middle. If 4 has used his dribble, X2 is relieved of this responsibility and can move out and cut off the outlet pass to 2, as shown in Diagram 10-21.

With the single adjustment of one player, X2, 4 could be double-teamed in the corner as shown in Diagram 10-22.

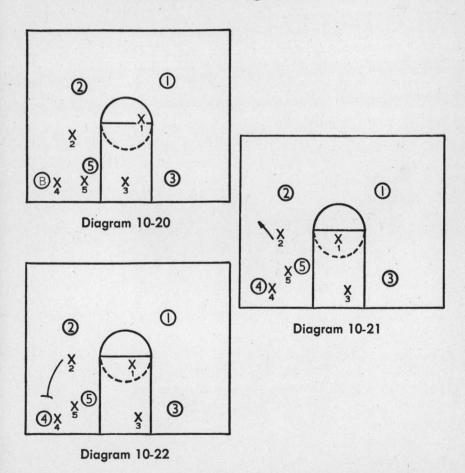

Diagram 10-20

Diagram 10-21

Diagram 10-22

The most effective corner stunt involves adjustments by X2 and X1. Diagram 10-23 illustrates X2 trapping 4 in the corner, and X1 sliding over to cut off the outlet pass to 2. This stunt must be predetermined in order for X1 to cheat toward 2 and be able to get to the cut-off position quickly.

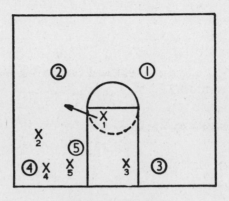

Diagram 10-23

Diagram 10-24 illustrates an inherent weakness with this stunt. X3 is the only defensive player in good rebound position. X5 must wheel inside of 5 to gain rebounding position. X1 and X4 must hustle to the board to help control the rebound when 4 shoots out of the corner.

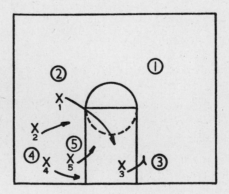

Diagram 10-24

11

Utilizing the Man-for-Man in Auxiliary Defensive Situations

Grouped under the heading of auxiliary plays are those special situations involving jump balls, free throws and out-of-bounds plays. The team defensive plan must include a basic method of defensing each of these situations. The time alloted to these situations during practice sessions should be in proportion to the frequency that they occur in the course of a game. Many young coaches have a tendency to spend entirely too much time developing special offensive plays for jump ball and out-of-bounds situations and fail to adequately cover how to defense these special plays.

Out-of-Bounds Under the Basket

The most dangerous out-of-bounds situation occurs when the ball is awarded to the opponent under his basket. Most teams have elaborate offensive formations with many optional plays from each for this situation. Diagram 11-1 illustrates perhaps the most common, and one of the most effective out-of-bounds plays used under the basket. This formation is referred to as a box. The defensive man assigned to the player making the throw-in should line up in a position in the lane between his man and the basket. Diagram 11-2 illustrates this position

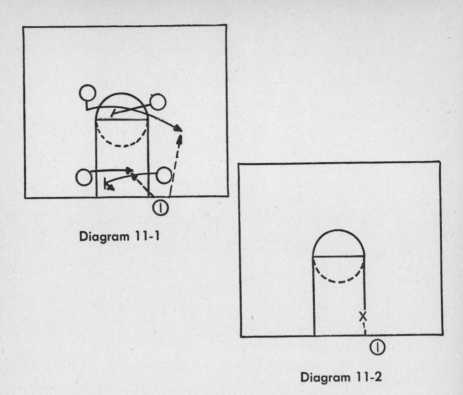

Diagram 11-1

Diagram 11-2

which is maintained in order to prevent 1 from making the throw-in, and then stepping inbounds under the basket for a return pass. From this position X1 can help his teammates should a player break loose for the pass inbounds.

Most out-of-bounds plays under the basket are designed to produce a layup or close shot. Bearing this in mind, the defense should make preventing the layup or close shot its first objective. Preventing the pass inbounds, directly underneath the basket, can best be accomplished by massing the defense in this area. Diagram 11-3 illustrates the defense sagging back under the basket on the out-of-bounds play.

Playing in this manner will invite the long pass out to 2 or 3. Should this pass be made, then the defense can come out under control and pick up their assigned man. Each defensive man should be in an open stance so that he can see more of the court as well as the ball. Warning a teammate of the impending screen and providing help is essential in defensing the out-of-bounds play. A defensive breakdown could result in a cheap basket.

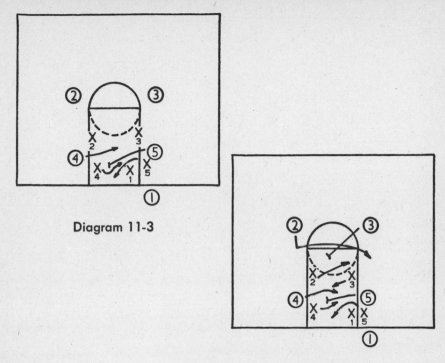

Diagram 11-3

Diagram 11-4

As 5 moves across to screen X4 in Diagram 11-4, X5 must warn X4 about the screen. X5 should loosen up and maintain a position between 5 and the ball as 5 moves across the lane. Loosening up also provides room for X4 to slide through the screen and keep his position between 4 and the ball. X1 is ready to help on any pass to a player under the basket. X2 and X3 crowd the lane area in an effort to force the long pass out to one of their men.

The offense would like to get a layup from the out-of-bounds play; however, the primary objective on all out-of-bounds situations is to insure a safe pass inbounds within the allotted five seconds provided by the rules. If 1 has not made the pass inbounds within three seconds, he looks for secondary passes. After three seconds have expired, each defensive player should be properly positioned on his assigned man. The defense will have a good opportunity to deflect or intercept the pass if, after jamming the basket area, they move quickly into a new intercepting position on their man. In Diagram 11-5 the original play has been stymied, and all the defensive players, except X1, close out

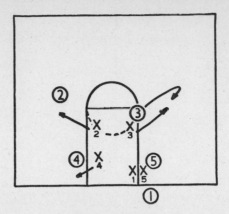

Diagram 11-5

on their assigned men. Offensive players have a tendency to run the play as taught to them with the full expectancy of its being successful. Many players, after carrying out their assignment, will not take the individual initiative to get open for the pass inbounds.

In situations that warrant such strategy the defense can apply pressure tactics against out-of-bounds plays under the opponent's basket. Diagram 11-6 illustrates the alignment of the defensive players when the strategy dictates that the pass inbounds be prevented or intercepted. Each player is in more of a closed stance, focusing greater attention on his man. The defensive man guarding the screener should call the screen. X5 and X2 should warn their teammates to watch the screen. X3 and X4 normally would slide through between the screener

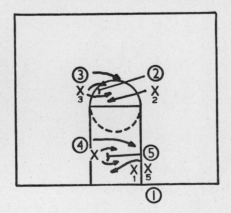

Diagram 11-6

and their teammates in this situation. X4 is given the option of sliding through the screen or, when the screener leaves plenty of room, going over the top of the pick.

Many defensive teams automatically jump into a zone each time the opponent is awarded the ball out-of-bounds under their goal. The principle of playing a zone in this situation is to mass the defense under the basket and force a long pass out to one of the guards. The zone also combats the offensive screens effectively, further reducing the possibility of a layup being scored.

Out-of-Bounds at Mid-Court

The team that is awarded the ball out-of-bounds at mid-court ordinarilly has an out-of-bounds play for the situation. In many cases the offense is content to successfully complete the inbounds pass and set up their regular offense. The defense has the option of conceding the pass inbounds and picking up in the regular defense or of playing the out-of-bounds situation the same as a tight situation.

Diagram 11-7 illustrates the defense setting up in a ten defense on the throw-in at mid-court. The pass inbounds is conceded and pressure is applied when the ball is moved in to the scoring area.

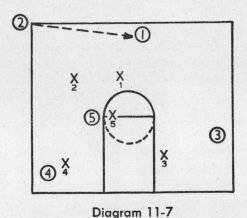

Diagram 11-7

Diagram 11-8 shows the alignment for a 50 defense. 2 is covered with the techniques that apply to a dribbler who has used his dribble. Unlike the inbounds tight situation, X2 cannot apply as much pressure

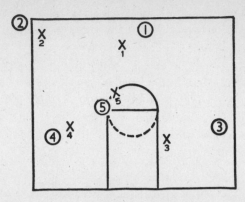

Diagram 11-8

on 2. X2 is restrained by the sideline, and 2 has the freedom of backing up out-of-bounds in order to allow himself more operating room. The freedom from aggressive pressure will make it easier for 2 to find his potential pass receivers and to complete the pass. Since there is no threat of a drive, X1 can close out on 1 and pressure him. X4 and X5 play the passing lanes, and X3 can drop off under the basket when 3 is two passes removed from the ball.

The defense has one definite advantage when the ball is out-of-bounds at mid-court, and that is that the ball is approximately 50 feet from the basket. 2 in many cases will be forced to make a long pass inbounds. Long passes made by 2 will provide the defense additional time to react in order to deflect or intercept the pass.

The defense, picking up at mid-court, should expect the offense to run special out-of-bounds plays. The type of out-of-bounds plays the offense will run against a half-court man-for-man defense will usually be based on the give and go, backdoor plays, blind screens from the rear, and lob passes.

An out-of-bounds situation at any other place on the court is covered by the team defense in accordance with the number of the defense in effect at the time the ball is awarded to the opponents.

Free Throw Alignment and Assignments

The alignment and assignment of players when the opponents are shooting a free throw is very important. Diagram 11-9 illustrates posi-

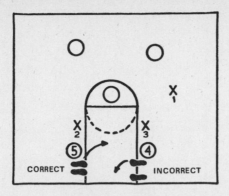

Diagram 11-9

tions of the defensive players along the lane. The rules provide that the inside positions be occupied by the defense. The two best rebounders should be stationed in these positions. A close game can be lost by 5 or 4 scoring a field goal after rebounding a missed free throw. In an effort to prevent this from happening, the inside defensive players are required to remind each other to block out prior to each free throw attempt. Notice the foot position of the defensive players occupying the inside position. The player responsible for blocking out 5 has his feet close together and at the uppermost part of the space provided for him. When he steps into the lane to block out 5, he pivots on the foot nearest the baseline, his right foot, and steps across in front of 5 with his left foot. The position of his pivot foot places him farther up the lane when he blocks out and allows him to control a greater area when contesting 5 for the rebound. 4, on the other hand, is allowed to get closer to the basket because of the incorrect footwork of the man assigned to block him out.

The first two spaces on each side of the free throw lane must be occupied with the defense in the inside positions, and the offense in the second spaces. The defense has the option to fill the third positions if they desire. In order to prevent the offense from getting the long rebound, or a rebound tapped back toward the shooter by 5 or 4, the defense should fill these positions. X1, in Diagram 11-9, is responsible for reminding X3 to block off the shooter. If X1 were on the opposite side of the court, he would inform X2, "You've got the shooter."

In the majority of cases the shooter will hit the free throw, which means that there will be no rebound. It is unwise for the defensive players to become eager and risk a lane violation, especially on the first of a bonus free throw situation.

Jump Ball Situations

The factors warranting consideration in held ball situations are many. There are three jumping areas: the center circle, the free throw circle at the offensive end of the court, and the one at the defensive end. The jump may involve two jumpers of equal size and jumping ability, or it may present an advantage or a disadvantage situation. the position on the court in which the jump will take place, and the possible control of the jump, present nine possibilities as far as strategy is concerned. Special scoring plays and plays designed to insure possession of the ball add to the possibilities. Defensive formations and tactics further complicate an already complex problem. Jump ball situations present the coach a real temptation to make the mistake of overcoaching.

The defensive aspects of jump ball situations involve either a plan to gain control of the tip or a special formation or plan designed to prevent the opponents from scoring on a fast break from the jump.

The team that finds itself at a disadvantage can utilize unorthodox alignments and special defensive schemes around the jumping circle that involve the knifing and rotating of the players in an effort to gain control of the ball. Many coaches play various alignments on the circle with three men and have one man back as a standing safety. The formation of the jumper, the three men on the circle, and the safety take various forms, e.g., "T", "Y", "◊", etc., and are named accordingly. These defensive formations are used during center jumps and jumps at the free throw circle opposite the goal the opponent is attacking, when it is apparent the opponent is going to control the tip.

Playing a safety man 15 or 20 feet off the jump circle removes all doubt as to who will control the tip. Teams that line up in this manner do so in order to prevent the fast break scoring play.

Diagram 11-10 illustrates four men lined up on the circle, each in position to contest his man for control of the tip, and it further illustrates how to protect against the fast break. 5 controls the tip and taps the ball to 4. X4 plays the ball since it was tapped in his direction. X4 should tap the ball toward a teammate when he can get a piece of it. X1 would move into the area in which the ball is tapped and play the ball

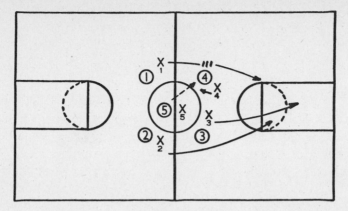

Diagram 11-10

as he retreats to the defensive basket. The moment the direction of the tap is determined to be away from them, X3 and X2 break immediately for the defensive goal. Playing in this manner will give the defense an opportunity to control a poorly placed tip, an uncontrolled tip, and a fumble by the receiver. On all jump ball situations four men should be on the circle. Play the ball if it is tipped in your direction. When the ball is tipped away from you, hustle back on defense.

The rules provide that each player is entitled to his position on the jump circle. Two players of the same team cannot line up shoulder to shoulder if the opponent desires a position between them. The only time an official will require a player to move or change his position is when this situation occurs. It becomes important then to line up quickly in certain spots on the circle in order to keep the opponent from occupying them. Diagram 11-11 illustrates a jump ball situation in front of the opponent's basket. Assuming that the opponent will control the tip, the most favored position for a teammate of the jumper would be directly in front of the jumper. This spot is indicated in the diagram with a square. This spot is usually occupied by the center, or if he is jumping, by the biggest player who is not jumping. The defense can prevent an easy basket by beating the opponents to this position directly in front of the basket and preventing them from occupying it.

Should the opponents gain this position, the defense will be obligated to play a man on both sides of this potential receiver, as shown in Diagram 11-12. In this situation the defense has no choice but to leave

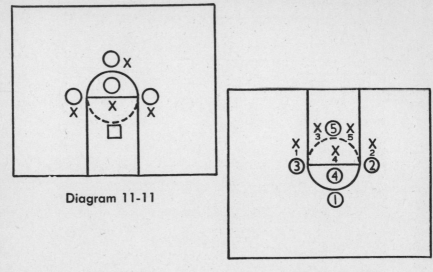

Diagram 11-11

Diagram 11-12

an opponent open to receive the tap. The man left uncovered should be the back man, 1, and the opposition should be encouraged to tip away from their basket.

The simplest method of dealing with a defensive jump ball situation is for each defensive man to line up with his assigned man, between him and the basket. Diagram 11-13 illustrates the defensive positions of each of the players on the circle. Each player on the circle goes after the ball if it is tipped towards him—otherwise, he retreats quickly to the defensive end of the court.

Diagram 11-14 illustrates a held ball between X1 and 3. X1, who is jumping, is responsible for making certain that his teammate, X3, covers his man for him on the jump. X1 and X3 must stay with the men they have on the jump until it is convenient to switch back to their original men.

When the defense deems it necessary to cover one man on the circle with two defensive players, one man must be left open. The opponent who will not be covered is determined by the position in which he is lined up. Diagram 11-15 illustrates the most awkward spot for a right-handed jumper to tip the ball. It is difficult for a player tipping with his right hand to turn the palm of his hand in such a way that it faces the area indicated in the diagram. A left-handed tipper would have the most difficulty tipping the ball into the back left area.

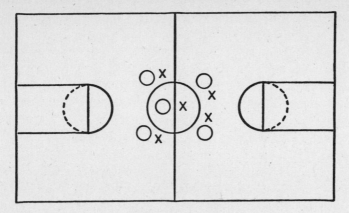

Diagram 11-13

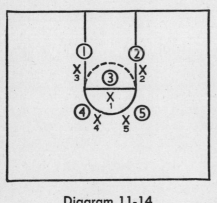

Diagram 11-14

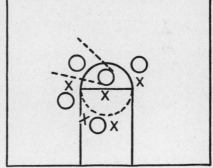

Diagram 11-15

Do not concede the tip. Play four men on the circle. Watch the jumper for signs that might give away his intentions. Watch the jumper's eyes especially, as they will sometimes betray his intentions. Listen for names and numbers and learn to associate them with specific plays or tipping lanes.

Auxiliary plans and defenses should be introduced and explained in early season, then practiced during scrimmages. Special games can be devised such that play is begun with a jump ball situation, a free throw, or an out-of-bounds situation.

Games and special rules for scrimmages can be devised that present opportunities for extra practice on auxiliary situations. For instance, a half-court scrimmage could be played with rules that stipulate that each time a team scores, it is awarded the ball out-of-bounds under the basket. These special rules could be changed to award the man who scored the field goal a free throw, or, after a basket, play could begin with a jump ball, etc. The coach who officiates full-court scrimmages can set up auxiliary plays as he deems necessary. The defense must be prepared for each of the situations, and the plan used should be simple and as similar to the regular defense as possible. Guard against over-coaching and spending too much practice time on these situations.

12

Rebounding in the Man-for-Man Defense

Rebounding is second only to defense as a factor contributing to winning basketball games. There is great truth in the slogan "The team that controls the boards controls the game."

Rebounding Statistics

As basketball becomes more sophisticated, the real value of rebounding becomes more apparent. Total individual rebounds was for years the only rebounding statistic kept. Then statisticians began to break the rebounds down into offensive and defensive rebounds. This breakdown provided a tremendous aid for the coach. Often players lack the height and jumping ability to be effective offensive rebounders. There is no reason however, for a team which is willing to work diligently in order to perfect the technique of boxing out, not to be a great defensive rebounding team. Many coaches fall into the trap of assuming that because their players are tall, strong, and can jump, they will automatically be outstanding rebounders, and that their team will be able to dominate the backboards. There is a direct correlation between the emphasis placed on rebounding, and the percentage of rebounds a team recovers. Coaches recognizing the lack of height and

jumping ability on their squad tend to place special emphasis on rebounding, especially defensive rebounding. They are often surprised to
discover that all too frequently the statistics indicate that teamwise the
smaller players are better defensive rebounders. The smaller players
block out better and cut down on the opponent's offensive rebounds
simply because they have been made to understand the importance of
doing so, and have been drilled extensively in the skills required.

Rebounding statistics are commonly kept on each individual with
the deserving recognition awarded for high honors. As a system of
checks and balances, the statistician can total the individual rebounds
and add to this the "team" rebounds. This total should be equal to the
number of shots missed. Team rebounds are rebounds which are not
controlled by an individual player, but one that caroms out of bounds.
Free throws missed, when the ball is dead and awarded to the shooter
for the second shot, are also classified as team rebounds.

Rebounding statistics are currently kept on a team percentage of
the total rebounds available. An analysis of the teams that consistently
capture the majority of the rebounds indicates that they are the teams
with the best winning percentage. A team that can control approximately 60 percent of the rebounds can be deficient in other areas of the
game, such as field goal percentage, excessive turnovers, poor free
throw shooting, and excessive fouling, and still win.

The follow-up shot coming from an offensive rebound, and offensive tip-ins, are classic examples of cheap baskets. Every effort must
be made to limit the opposition to only one shot each time they gain
possession of the basketball.

Requisites for Rebounding

Players with certain physical attributes have a distinct advantage
in rebounding. Tall players obviously have an advantage over shorter
players. A player's height can be deceptive. The coach should take
notice of the player's body-build as it relates to his neck and his arms.
Many players who are measured as tall, in reality have long necks
which offer little advantage in the game of basketball. Often a player
with no neck, that is, his head sits on his shoulders, can, as far as the
game is concerned, be considered several inches taller than his actual
height.

Many tall players have short arms. As a rule of thumb, you can check the length of a player's arms by measuring his arm span from finger tips to finger tips, while he is standing with his toes and chest against a wall and his arms parallel with the floor. His arm span, thusly measured, should be equivalent to his height. A comparison of these two measurements will give the coach a good idea of the athlete's playing height. Another measurement which will prove more helpful than actual height in evaluating a player's physical attributes is measurement of his standing reach. This measurement can be taken by standing the player facing against the wall and measuring that point on the wall which he can reach while standing flat-footed.

Height as a factor in rebounding is indeed important, but quite possibly it has been overemphasized. Strength and weight have become recognized as major factors in rebounding. A player not only has to gain the proper rebounding position, but must have the weight and muscle to keep that position when the opponents are applying great amounts of pressure against him. The higher the level of competition, the more the officials permit contact underneath the boards. The advantage of extra pounds increases proportionately with the amount of contact permitted.

Jumping ability is an asset in rebounding. This ability must be fused with the all-important ingredient of timing. Inexperienced players have a tendency to jump too soon when rebounding. Only through practice and constant reminding by the coach can this tendency be overcome. Many players jump especially high on their first leap after the ball, but, when they are unsuccessful, they fail to make the second and third attempts. These "one time Charleys" sometimes jump so haphazardly that they land off the court or behind the backboard. Each jump should be concluded by hitting the floor with the feet spread, the knees flexed, and the arms up ready to go right back up for another attempt for the rebound. As a player jumps the second, third, and fourth time, the height of his jump usually decreases with each jump. A good drill designed to improve stamina and to increase the height of the jumps when several are made consecutively is to station a player underneath the goal and have him alternate hands touching the goal first with the left hand, then on the next jump with the right hand, etc. Using an adjustable rebounding machine or some other target for the players to touch, and setting it at a height that will challenge each individual, will improve the drill.

Many coaches utilize an off-season and/or pre-season weight training program for their players to develop strength, add weight, and increase endurance. A basic weight program has proven especially helpful for the tall uncoordinated youngsters who lack endurance, and who cannot work with their arms extended above their head for long periods of time.

An adapted weight program designed to improve jumping ability is used by many coaches for six or eight weeks prior to the beginning of the regular season. These exercises consist of weight resistance activities—for example, the player does calisthentics, for developing the legs, with weight on his shoulders. Heel raises, knee bends, straddle hops, and hopping are weight resistance exercises that have proven to increase the height which a player can jump.

It is difficult for players to form the habit of keeping their arms and hands up prior to going for a rebound. Much of the problem relates to the discomfort which accompanies this position when it is maintained over a period of time. In addition to the weight program, an excellent developer of arm and hand strength is the medicine ball. One of the best drills with the medicine ball involves two players stationed on each side of the goal. The first player throws the ball high on the board in such a manner that it will rebound to the second player. The second player jumps high with both arms extended and rebounds the ball. He is allowed to come back to the floor, but he must keep his arms extended. He then jumps and puts the ball in the basket. The second player then passes off the backboard to the first player who rebounds and scores while keeping his arms extended above his head.

Agility is an asset in rebounding. The more agile players can move quicker under control to the desired rebounding position. The ability to get directly underneath the ball, when possible, gives the rebounder added reach and makes him more effective as a rebounder. If the rebounder judges the flight of the rebound in such a way that he rebounds the ball directly over his head, he will have the advantage of an additional reaching height of several inches.

Spectators, teammates, and even the coach can be fooled into thinking that a player is a good rebounder because the few rebounds he gets are done in such a spectacular way. The apparently aggressive player, who goes high in the air in spread eagle fashion, gets the ball, and swings his elbows madly as he comes to the floor with a big bang is referred to as a T.V. rebounder. A quick check of the statistics do not agree with what one recalls about the game. The tendency is to remember those spectacular rebounds and leave the gym thinking "that

guy is a great rebounder,'' when in fact, his rebounds can be counted
on one hand. Usually the T. V. rebounders are not adept at making the
outlet pass and getting the fast break started, but rather prefer to
massage the ball making sure that they hold it long enough for
everyone to see who just made the big play. The guy who can grab the
rebound and clear the ball quickly from the congested basket area
consistently is the rebounder that is concentrating so much on getting
the ball that he does not have time to put on a show.

Blocking Out

Ideas regarding blocking out, or boxing out as it is referred to by
some, have changed radically in recent years. Fifteen or twenty years
ago coaches were pretty much in agreement as to the technique that
should be used to most effectively keep the offensive players off the
boards. As in most other phases of the game, coaches have tried new
approaches with varying degrees of success. Regardless of the particular technique involved, there is general agreement concerning the basic
principles involved in boxing the offensive player off the boards. To
begin with, the defensive player must play his man first, then the ball.
In order to effectively block out, the defensive player must check the
offensive player to determine the direction in which he moves in approaching the basket. Position is basic in blocking out. The defensive
player should always maintain a position on the floor between his man
and the basket. When this location on the court is correct, the defensive
player should always be on the inside position. With the advantage of
being closer to the backboard than his opponent, the defensive player
should be able to beat his man to the ball.

When a defensive player is matched up against an opponent that is
several inches taller than he is, it is more important that he make
contact and keep it for a greater period of time. When such a mis-
match occurs in an area close to the basket, it is recommended that the
defensive player concentrate all his effort on blocking out and pay little
attention to the ball. In such cases the smaller defender is making a
greater team contribution by making certain that his taller opponent is
not released and cannot rebound the missed shot. Frequently, the tall-
est player or the best rebounder on the opponent's team is blocked out
in this manner. When this method is used, the responsibility for getting
the rebound rests with his four teammates.

There are several methods that coaches teach in blocking the opponent off the boards. In order that each may be described, we will call them the close check, the loose check and open check.

To utilize the close check the defensive player must be very close to his opponent when the shot is taken. This method of blocking out is easiest to use on the shooter because of the proximity of the defender to the shooter. If other players away from the shooter use this method, they must go to their assigned opponent and get close enough to him to make this method effective. When the shot is taken, the defender touches the offensive rebounder in the stomach with his extended hand, then makes a 180 degree pivot into the opponent. The defender must have a very wide stance, his knees flexed, and his upper arm extended with the elbows out. As the player blocking out makes his front pivot, he should contact the opponent with his tail. He must keep this contact for several seconds by sliding or shuffling his feet in such a direction that it counters the effort of the offensive player trying to get around him. The extended elbows enlarge the blocking out surface and help the defender to maintain contact.

The primary difference in the close check and the loose check is the kind of pivot used by the defender. When using the loose check to block out, the defender watches his man to determine the direction of his path to the basket, then reverse pivots in his path, making contact. He retains this position, using the shuffle step and the extended elbows to maintain contact, until he determines the direction in which the ball will rebound. Finally, he releases the contact and goes for the ball.

The open check can be compared to the open defensive stance used when covering a man away from the ball. In this instance the defender backs off slightly, and opens up his stance in such a way that, momentarily, he can see both the ball in flight to the basket and the man he is to block out. From this position he moves into the path of the offensive player, makes contact, releases, and goes for the ball.

In rare instances, when the offensive player is an outstanding offensive rebounder, the coach may be concerned enough to designate a defensive player who concentrates his efforts on keeping this man off the boards. A completely closed stance, with no pivot whatsoever, can be effective in these special cases. The defender simply face guards the offensive rebounder as he approaches the boards. The defender in this case completely ignores the ball and devotes his full attention to blocking the offensive man in order to prevent him from going to the boards.

It then becomes the responsibility of the other four defenders to capture the rebound.

Reacting to the Direction of the Ball

To block out or not to block out is the question. In recent years the trend has been away from blocking out and special emphasis has been placed on quickness and reacting to the direction of the rebound. The advent of the integration movement brought about many changes in coaches' philosophies of how the game should be played. The leaping ability and lightning quickness that many of the black athletes possess has been a big factor in coaches' ideas concerning blocking out. In the final analysis, all coaches should be interested in results, and if a player can get the job done using techniques that differ from the coach's ideas, it should be of little consequence. The intelligent coach will recognize the results obtained by using new approaches to any phase of the game, and he not only will encourage the use of such tactics, but he will learn all that he can from his players in order to be better prepared to help other players.

If a coach believes that certain of his players are possessed with the innate ability to react to the direction in which the ball rebounds, then the primary teaching responsibility will involve the defensive players' position on the court. The defense has a built-in advantage in rebounding because they have the inside position. It is not necessary to block out to the extent that the defensive player has contact with the offensive player, provided the defensive man maintains his position closer to the ball when it is on the backboard. If the defensive man has the advantage of being closer to the ball—and *reacts quickly to the ball*—he will beat the offensive player to the ball and gather in the rebound.

This technique of positioning and reacting works best when the defensive player is assigned to a player on the perimeter of the offense. If the offensive player is close to the basket, it is best to make contact with him while blocking out.

Forming a cup or triangle near the basket is the team rebounding concept used by many coaches. When the offense takes a shot at the basket, the three defenders nearest the basket, usually the biggest and strongest players on the team, move into predetermined positions near the goal. These three players assume a spread position on the court, taking up as much space as possible. They attempt to get close enough together so that the offensive rebounders cannot split them. The two outside players not in the triangle move into areas near the junction of the free throw line and the lane on either side of the court. These players are responsible for long rebounds toward the foul line and for those that rebound into the corners. Diagram 12-1 illustrates the positions of all five players when the defensive cup is formed.

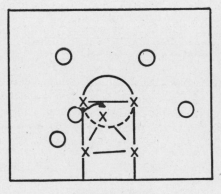

Diagram 12-1

In each of the blocking out methods except face guarding, the defender checks his man first, then finds the ball. The quickness with which he reacts to the ball will be a major factor in the success he has as a rebounder.

Rather than insist on blocking out with contact and pressure applied to the offensive player, many coaches insist only on position and emphasize reaction toward the ball. The defensive player has the position advantage when the ball is shot. If he makes whatever adjustment on the court that is necessary to keep the inside position, and then reacts quickly to the ball, he will recover the rebound.

Basketball supposedly is a noncontact game. The aggressive play and excessive contact that takes place under the boards contradicts this statement. At higher levels of competition the officials permit more contact. Aggressiveness and determination then become major factors in successful rebounding. The following true story will illustrate the importance of determination rebounding. Several years ago there was a basketball player at Southern Methodist University by the name of Joel Krog. Joel was about 6′ 4″ tall and not an exceptional jumper, but he managed to break the school record in rebounding. When reporters from the Dallas newspapers asked him how he managed this feat, his reply was, "I have but one rule, I try to get them all."

Some teams play their offense such that designated players, usually the guards, are assigned the responsibility of playing safety. When these teams shoot the ball, the three tall inside men go to the offensive boards, and the guards are designated to balance the court and stop the fast break. When the scouting report indicates that certain players do not crash the offensive boards, the defenders assigned to guard them can ignore the blocking out and go for the ball.

Each coach, in determining what plan of rebounding he will use, should consider the specific abilities of the individual players. If a player is adept at reacting to the ball and can get the job done, it might be a mistake to spend a great deal of time teaching him to block out. The coach should guard against overcoaching a player that is a natural rebounder. Any team can be a good defensive rebounding team if all five players either block out or react quickly and aggressively to the ball.

13

Employing Man-for-Man
Defensive Strategy

The basic man-for-man defense is designed to combat
the offensive situations most often confronted, as well as those that
may be seen less frequently, but that pose a special problem. The basic
defense is a blend of pressure and sag that should be sufficient for the
vast majority of situations. Special offensive strategies must be dealt
with by using variations of the basic defense.

The coach must make a determination in terms of the size, speed,
quickness, experience, etc. of this team, as to how much pressure he
can apply. Those years in which the team is blessed with speed and
quickness, it would be a wise decision to use a 95 defense after each
goal and to drop back in a 50 when the opponents gain possession by
rebounding, etc. If the coach happened to be blessed with a group of
tall players, it might be advisable to set up in a 50 defense each time it
loses possession of the ball.

Once the bread and butter defensive plan is established, it should
be the defense used in the majority of instances. If a team is going into
the game "blind," that is, with little or no information about the
opponent, it should begin the game with its best defense. In these cases
the coach and players will have to scout the opponent as the game
proceeds, and make adjustments accordingly. It is a good idea to vary

the defense for short periods of time during the first half. The coach should pay particular attention to the offensive reaction to these variations, and he can then be in a better position to determine the best variations to use toward the end of the game if it becomes necessary.

If a scouting report is available on the opponent, variations of the basic defense can be set up and practiced in preparation for this opponent. On those occasions when the coach feels that a special concocted defense might be necessary for a certain opponent, such a defense can be set up as plan B. The bread and butter defense should be tried, and only when it is unsuccessful, should the team revert to the secondary defense. Occassionally there will be players on the team who, because of lack of speed or some other reason, are not adept at playing the bread and butter defense. The occasion that warrants substituting them into the game for a regular might present a situation where the defense could be changed when the substitute enters the game.

If the defense finds itsclf in a tough ball game and is steadily dropping bchind in the score, it is not wise to resort to drastic measures early in the game. A time-out during which the team can regroup, and the coach can encourage them and make suggestions for improvements would be in order. If things fail to improve, the coach should use a time-out to remind the team of the tight situations that can be capitalized on in an effort to gain possession of the ball. The next area of emphasis the coach should stress is the double-team opportunities which present themselves. At this point, if the defense does not tighten up, the coach should resort to substitution as a means of plugging the weak spots. If the situation gets worse, the coach can vary the defense by picking up farther from the basket, e.g., change from a 50 to a 75 defense. Should these defensive adjustments fail to produce the desired results, there is little left but to resort to the catch-up defense described later in this chapter.

It is a wise coach who guards against wasting his time-outs. Many times communications with the players can be made from the bench. It is helpful if, during free throw situations a designated guard comes into the playing area near the bench in order to receive instructions from the coach. Many times the coach needs to talk to only one player, and it is not advisable to call a time-out early in the game for this purpose. The time-out can be saved by substituting for the player involved. The coach can relate his instructions and put the regular back on the court.

A manager or assistant coach should keep an accurate account of the number of fouls on each player when they are not recorded on the scoreboard. Fouling not only sends the opponent to the free throw line with the opportunity to put points on the board, but it has a greater implication in that it can disqualify key players. The first move by the coach to prevent a player from fouling out would be to change his defensive assignment to a less active opponent. When the player in foul trouble is a key player and must be in the game, it would be advisable to go into the sagging variation of the basic defense or even resort to a zone. The offensive strategy of many teams is built around running their offense at a given player with the intention of disqualifying him or adversly effecting his play by getting him into foul trouble.

The defensive-minded coach will substitute for players who are not carrying out their defensive responsibilities. Sending a player to the scoring table to report into the game when a player commits a glaring mistake is one of the best motivating factors to encourage good defense. If a player, any player, is removed from the game for committing certain cardinal sins on defense, the team will understand that the coach is serious about defense. The team must be made to understand that the coach is not giving lip service to the subject of defense, but that he believes that defense wins games. After a few victories the team will be convinced and even become enthusiastic about defense.

Combating the Delay Game

The term *delay* is used to describe those teams who play a deliberate, ball control type of game. This disciplined, pattern-type offense ensures them that they are on offense during the majority of the game. This style of play requires that they pass the basketball ten or fifteen times before they shoot. Teams using this kind of offense end up with outstanding defensive statistics not necessarily because their defense is so great, but because they keep the opponents from scoring by controlling and keeping possession of the ball for most of the game.

The success the ball control teams enjoy relates directly to the success they have in controlling the tempo of the game. Their objective is not only to maintain prolonged possession of the ball, but also to set the pace at which the game will be played. Teams that ordinarily utilize the fast break discover that they are so pleased to finally gain possession of the ball that they tend to overprotect it, and consequently, fall into the trap of playing the other guy's game. The teams that run a delayed offense have another advantage over most teams because they are usually extremely well-disciplined. The slow-down teams are at their best when they pass the ball ten or twelve times and score on a high percentage shot and then have the opponents rush up the court and give up the ball by taking a hurried shot.

The ball control teams normally do not win by big margins. They are used to playing close games and function better in these situations than less-disciplined teams do. Ball control teams sometimes fool the opposition into thinking that the defense is so tough that they cannot get an open shot. Actually, these teams do not take the first or necessarily the second open shot they get, because they believe that they can get that same shot or a better one *at the time they* want to put the ball up.

Ball control, or the delay game, is one of the best equalizers for teams with inferior material. If they can keep the score close, they always have a chance of winning in the final minutes. These same teams, when their personnel is superior, stand a greater chance of being upset.

The basic man-for-man defense is designed to combat the stalling-type offenses. When the defense sags or plays a dropback zone, the ball control team has no problem holding on to the ball as long as they want. If this same team comes out and applies pressure, it is quite possible that, because this is a special defense that is seldom practiced, the ball control team can get by it for easy baskets. The philosophy behind the regular man-for-man defense is to play, as a basic defense, the kind of defense that would be most effective against the ball control team. The basic man-for-man defense must be played with the same pride and determination that the offense puts into its effort to control the ball. It is a matter of who is going to make a mistake first, the offense or the defense. The team that is willing and capable of playing sustained defense over a period of time must also have the intelligence and patience necessary to get a good shot each time it gains the ball.

The Catch-Up Defense

As the name of the defense implies, the catch-up defense is a desperation measure that is used as a last resort. In those instances in which time is running out, and you find yourself on the short end of the score, it becomes necessary to do something, even if it is wrong. Most coaches would prefer to lose by a wide margin trying to win, rather than sit back and lose by a few points.

The opponents have a lead, they have the ball in their front court, and time is running out. The defense must make every effort to gain possession of the ball. The offense will be spread over the entire half court with the objective of maintaining possession of the ball or shooting an unmolested layup. This offensive tactic is referred to as a "freeze" as opposed to the delay game. The best chance the defense will have to get the ball is when an offensive player picks up his dribble. The dribbler should be rushed, and the other four players should get in the passing lanes and go after the next pass. The defensive player covering the ball handler must prevent him from making a good backdoor pass. The catch-up defense is a desperation defense and is the only defense in which the defense gambles and takes chances.

A well-organized offense will spread out and pass the ball against a double-teaming defense. The defense should choose their opportunities to double-team and not let the offense run them to death chasing the ball. Anytime your man takes you close to the ball, you should double up on the ball handler. If an offensive player dribbles toward a teammate—double. If an offensive player screens for a teammate —double up on the ball handler. Any time two defensive players double-team the ball, the three remaining players must rotate to pick up the potential pass receivers. The double-team could be affected in several ways, and it must involve alert anticipation by the three rotating players. Diagram 13-1 illustrates X1 leaving his man to double-team the ball handler, 2. X4 must protect the sideline pass to 4, and X5 fronts 5. X3 moves up to cut off the cross-court pass to 1.

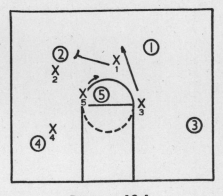

Diagram 13-1

A similar situation is shown in Diagram 13-2. In this instance, X5 is the logical man to cut off the cross-court pass, and X3 works to get the fronting position on 5. It will be noted that 3 could move into the lane and be open for a pass from 2. It is the responsibility of X2 and X1 to prevent such a pass. When the defense double-teams, there are not enough defensive players to put two on the ball, cut off the passing lanes, and protect the basket, too. In the catch-up defense the basket is left unguarded, and every effort is made to intercept the pass.

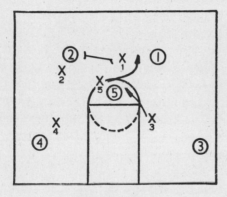

Diagram 13-2

Diagram 13-3 illustrates a common defensive trap, and the rotation involved. X4 moves up to trap with X2. X5 cuts off the sideline pass to 4. X3 moves up to cover 5, and X1 must protect against the cross-court pass.

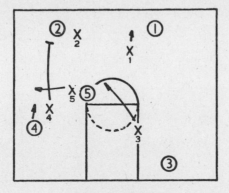

Diagram 13-3

There are many possibilities involved in double-teaming out of the catch-up defense. Extensive half-court scrimmage against the freeze is the only way to cover the many possibilities that exist. When the defense fails to recognize the opportunities to double-team, the coach should stop the scrimmage and have the defense walk through the trap and rotation in order to emphasize the possibilities that exist.

Against a freeze continuity that features a dribbler, the defense should keep continuous pressure on him in hopes of a closely guarded five-second violation. All defensive players should be alert to double on the dribbler if he dribbles near them.

When the offense is successfully holding the ball in the mid-court area, the defensive player assigned to the ball handler should overplay the ball handler and encourage him to dribble toward the basket. Diagram 13-4 illustrates this defensive move and shows how this forcing action will put the dribbler in a position that will allow the defense to double-team him. The defense has a definite advantage when the ball is in the corners. The ball handler should be forced into these areas as often as possible. These corners are shown in Diagram 13-5. The

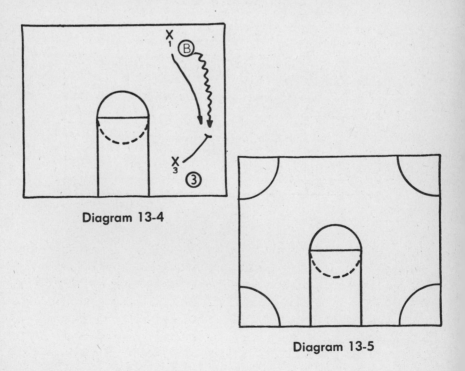

Diagram 13-4

Diagram 13-5

defense has more opportunities to stunt when the offense takes the ball deep toward the baseline. The corner stunts can be executed when the ball is deep in the corner. The offense should not be allowed to hold the ball. They should be forced to take it to the basket in an effort to shoot a layup. It is amazing how many crucial layups are missed in the freeze game.

The Full-Court Catch-Up Defense

Any time the ball is out-of-bounds, and the catch-up defense is being employed, the defense should be in a 100 or blitz defense. Each defender should play the passing lane and make every effort to prevent the pass from coming in to his man. If the inbounds pass is completed, the defense should immediately trap the ball with the nearest man. Diagram 13-6 illustrates a guard-forward sideline trap that occurs frequently when the blitz defense is employed. X2 tries for the intercep-

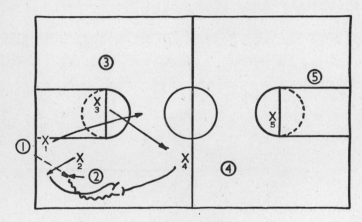

Diagram 13-6

tion and fails. 2 begins to dribble up the sideline, and X4 attacks the dribbler, trying to stop his dribble. Notice that X4 approaches 2 in the passing lane between 2 and 4. Should X4 run directly toward the ball, 2 will be able to pass quickly up the sideline to 4. X5 is the safety and must take care of the basket and, at the same time, protect against the long pass to 5. The rotation of the defense sends X3 to check the sideline pass, and X1 drops back into the middle to guard against a pass into that area. Should the position of 4 be deeper, the rotation would involve X5 cutting off the sideline pass, X3 covering the basket and/or post, and X1 checking the cross-court pass, as shown in Diagram 13-7.

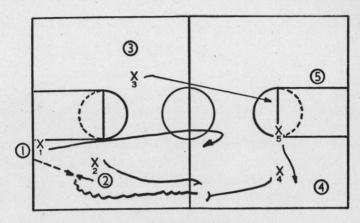

Diagram 13-7

Should 2 receive the ball and dribble into the middle of the court, X1 would aid X2 in setting the double-team. Diagram 13-8 illustrates the guard and guard double-team. The rotation of the other three men is determined by the position of the offensive players. X1 and X2 double-team. 1 is left open as long as he is behind the ball. X3, X4, and X5 must prevent the pass to their men. Diagram 13-9 shows 1

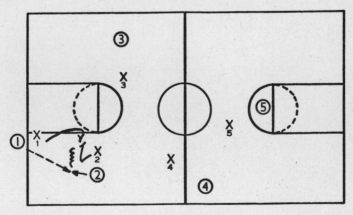

Diagram 13-8

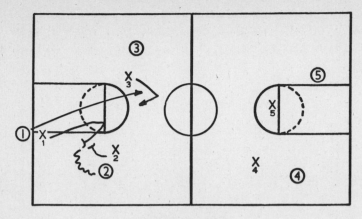

Diagram 13-9

moving upcourt after passing the ball inbounds. X3 in this instance must make a decision whether to guard 3 or 1. The rule is to take the man nearest the ball. Diagram 13-10 shows 1 moving to the sideline, on the ball side, ahead of the ball. In this instance X4 must cover the man nearest the ball, which would be 1.

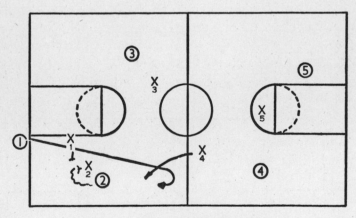

Diagram 13-10

Many offensive teams use the trailer extensively to beat the trapping press. 1 will pass the ball inbounds and then move toward, but behind, the ball for a return pass as shown in Diagram 13-11. The pass back to the trailer often gives him room to attack the defense quickly

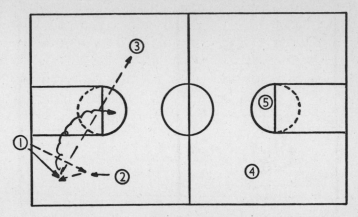

Diagram 13-11

with a dribble, or to pass the ball to 3 before the defense can react to the opposite side of the court. After X1 has double-teamed several times, it is a good risk to gamble on intercepting this return pass to 1, as shown in Diagram 13-12. Many times X1, or any other player moving into the double-team, can fake the trap and get the dribbler to pick up his dribble, then drop back into the passing lane to his original man. On other occasions, the defender can actually trap and retreat after the dribbler is dead. Anytime the ball handler can be forced to pick up his dribble, it is to the advantage of the defense if he is covered by only one man. The result then can be a tight situation with all potential receivers covered with pressure.

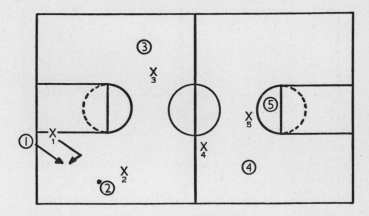

Diagram 13-12

If the offense attacks with a three-man front, the defense must trap with two of the three men defensing the offensive back line. Diagram 13-13 illustrates the impracticability of a front line and back line defensive player trapping against such an offensive act. X5 should not be expected to move across the court in time to cut off the pass to 4.

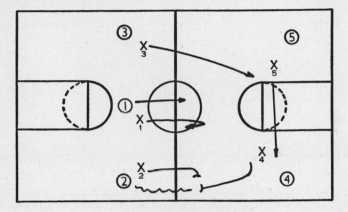

Diagram 13-13

Diagram 13-14 illustrates the proper defensive trap and cut-off position when the offense attacks with a three man front. X1 must get outside and prevent 1 from driving down the sideline. X2 moves in to set the trap, and X3 now takes the man nearest the ball, which is 2. X3 must protect the sideline if the ball comes to his side of the court, X2 would

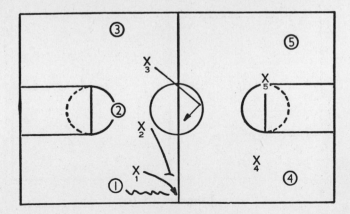

Diagram 13-14

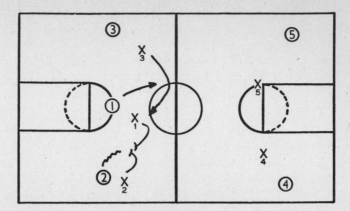

Diagram 13-15

double, and X1 would cut rotate to check the pass to 2. Diagram 13-15 illustrates the trap when the dribbler tries to split the defensive front line. X1 and X2 double when the dribbler drives between them. X3 rotates and cuts off the passing lane to the man nearest the ball, 1. Diagram 13-16 illustrates the rotation when 3 moves upcourt in front of the ball. Notice that X5 leaves 5 on the baseline and plays 3, who is the man nearest the ball.

The last resort for the defense is to deliberately foul an offensive player in order to stop the clock. The player fouled should be one of the poorer free throw shooters.

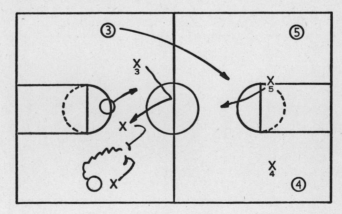

Diagram 13-16

The situations that call for the catch-up defense also require special offensive tactics. Once the defense gains possession of the ball, they must move it into scoring territory quickly and get a good shot. Taking a poor shot and missing nullifies the extra defensive effort it took to gain possession of the ball. Court balance, when the shot is taken, is now discarded, and all five players are sent to the offensive boards.

When each defensive player thoroughly understands the basic man-for-man defense, is willing to get down in a good stance, and play aggressive, hard-nosed defense, it will seldom be necessary to run the catch-up defense.

14

Summary of the Man-for-Man Defense

In summarizing the basic man-for-man defense, the most frequently committed mistakes are listed, the special areas and marking on the court are reviewed, and also, an outline of the basic rules governing the man-for-man defense is included.

Common Defensive Mistakes

Many coaches explain their team's defeat with expressions such as "We just couldn't hit tonight" or "We got the shots, but they wouldn't fall." This reasoning may be sound, but a few coaches prefer to take a long hard look at their team's defense and rebounding when analyzing the cause for a loss.

The defensive-minded coach can trace the vast majority of the opponent's scores directly to a defensive mistake. These coaches like to believe that their team can win even on the nights their shooting percentages are off. After losing a close game, the coach can recall literally scores of defensive mistakes, any one of which could have cost his team the ball game. Every team has those nights when they are cold offensively, but defense should be consistent.

Listed below are some of the most common defensive mistakes that players make while playing the basic man-for-man defense:

1. Permitting dribbler to get baseline or sideline.
2. Failure to block out.
3. Committing unnecessary foul.
4. Inadequate help on screens inside scoring area.
5. Lack of communication between players.
6. Failure to give front line support or help.
7. Insufficient pressure on passer.
8. Overpressing, gambling and taking chances.
9. Improper court balance.
10. Failure to force receiver to move to catch ball.
11. Permitting dribbler to get by the defensive man in full-court defense.
12. Poor defensive break.
13. Failure to rotate when defensive post picks up driver.
14. Failure to attack player with ball in shooting position.
15. Improper defensive position away from ball.
16. Turning back on ball (improper position and use of vision).

The two biggest defensive plays that can be made are: *drawing the charging foul* and *blocking a shot*.

Special Defensive Areas of the Court

The various areas of the court that merit special defensive consideration have been covered. These areas and other markings on the court that have special significance are shown in Diagram 14-1.

Outline of Basic Rules for Man-for-Man Defense

Listed below are some of the more important defensive rules on which the success of the basic man-for-man defense depends.

1. The farther your man is from the ball, the farther from him toward the ball you play.
2. Move in the direction the ball moves before your man does. This applies not only to the man covering the passer, but to

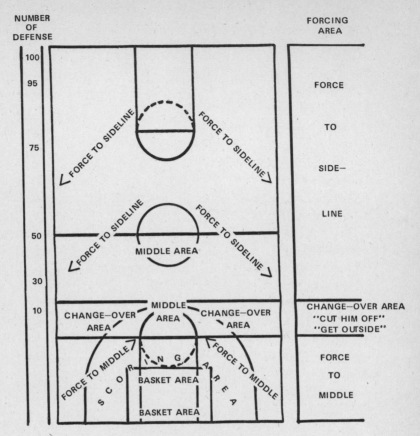

Diagram 14-1

all five defensive players. Move not only on passes, but when
the ball is dribbled, too.

3. Do not permit your man to stand still and receive a pass.
Make him move to get open.

4. Concentrate on these three things: (1) the ball, (b) your man
and (c) the middle.

   a. *The Ball*, so you will know when it is passed and dribbled, as that changes the position you take on your man.
You must know when it is shot to react to rebound
quickly. You have to know when it penetrates so you can
plug the middle.

b. *Your Man*, so that he won't lose you or position you. If he moves only a *foot*, it changes your position slightly.

c. *The Middle*, because it is your responsibility if an open driver comes in. Each player off the ball must be ready to help his teammate guarding the dribbler. Remember the man guarding the dribbler will always force him to the middle.

5. As long as the dribbler is alive, play more in the middle helping out. The objective is to stop the dribbler and then *get tight quick–(everyone yell "tight")*.

6. *Respect good passes*.

7. Do not press to the point that the dribbler gets by. Play the man, not the ball—bother them so they make the mistake.

8. Pressure the offense in front court enough so that they can't concentrate on pattern or get a good effective pass inside to pivot area. Don't let a man receive standing flat-footed —make him move toward the ball.

9. If your man does receive (it is impossible to keep him from doing so), make him receive away from you and the goal. They will eventually make an offensive mistake unless the defense goes to sleep first.

10. It is everyone's duty to always point the opponent's good player or players.

11. On screens outside the scoring area, slide through.

12. On screens on the ball inside the scoring area, go over the top.

13. On screens away from the ball, slide through.

14. Play for charge when the dribbler is going toward the goal, when you get the dribbler on a baseline, when helping on the lob pass, after the ball handler passes off on a three-on-one or two-on-one situation, and on a jump switch.

15. Don't cut off your man or try to do so too quickly. Remember your objective is to drive him to the baseline, then use the baseline as a helper. Most players will try to drive on between you and the baseline.

16. When the ball handlers penetrate with a quick drive, start backward movement long before they get to you and take more time driving them to the sideline.

17. Don't let a dribbler get deeper than any of you, and if the ball

is passed deeper than you, react to the ball quickly. Their men back of the ball are no threat.

18. Avoid being overanxious and using bad judgment by over-pressing trying to steal the ball.
19. If your man passes and moves toward the ball and on toward the basket, move first and make him go around you. Don't let him beat you to the receiving point in *shooting* territory.
20. A pressing defense can hurt defensive rebounding if the defense does not react to the ball quickly. Pressing places the defense farther from the basket and gives them a greater distance to move.
21. If they lob to pivot, that pass is *everyone's*—go get it.
22. Don't reach for the ball unless the dribbler does not have it protected. Don't lose balance reaching or lunging, or foul.
23. Talk, talk, and talk while on defense.
24. Apply as much pressure as you possibly can with respect to your ability and the ability of your man—*no more and no less*.
25. The whole idea is to make *them* make the *mistake*, keep them off pattern, and keep them from feeding their pivot men effectively.
26. A pressing defense is a *five-man proposition*.
27. Stay down and low and move your feet until the whistle blows.

This book has been designed for basketball coaches who are convinced that defense is at least equally important as offense. Much space has been devoted to the individual techniques involved in the man-for-man defense. These individual techniques and basic fundamentals are woven into the team aspect of defense. A complete system of defense, with variations and strategies, is presented as a possible solution to the many situations that will confront the defense. The slogan which hangs in many basketball dressing rooms expresses very well the philosophy behind the development of a tough, hard-nosed, basically sound defense. This slogan reads: "Offense wins reputations; Defense wins games."

Index

215

Z